Jeremiah

K.W. Bow

Copyright 2017 by Kenneth W. Bow
The book author retains sole copyright to
his contributions to this book.
Published 2017.
Printed in the United States of America.

All rights reserved.

No portion of this book may be reproduced, stored in a retrieval system, or transmitted in any form or by any means – electronic, mechanical, photocopy, recording, scanning, or other – except for brief quotations in critical reviews or articles, without the prior written permission of the author.

ISBN 978-1-946234-12-4

Cover art and design: Mark Gauthier.
Editor-in-chief: Susan Lind.

This book was published by BookCrafters,
Parker, Colorado.
www.bookcrafters.net

Foreword

Thank you reader, for selecting my book. There are many choices of books and we all have a limited window of time to read. I appreciate you purchasing my product. It is a humbling thing to know someone would choose to purchase, and then read your work. I do not take it as a small matter. By purchasing and reading a book, the reader and the author form a certain bond as they travel a road together for a short time. It is especially rewarding when the two agree on the content. It is my hope you can find inspiration and life challenges in the pages of this small booklet.

From the days of my high school years I have found the Bible fascinating. I have travelled to Israel on two occasions to learn more about the land and culture of the Bible. I worked on an archaeological dig and lived on a Kibbutz to better inform myself of how to understand this book from God. I have read it from cover to cover over twenty times, and it is still as exciting to me as it ever was.

The Bible is a magnificent journey and experience. It is ever a delight. In it you will travel to distant lands and meet some of the most incredible people of history. It will introduce you to kings and peasants. You will walk the palace halls of castles and the open fields of the countryside. You will meet the famous and be introduced to people whose name we will never know. You will read some of the greatest love stories ever told and you will see the dark side of man as the evil manifests itself in heinous ways. Every emotion of man is highlighted at some time. You will see greed and avarice and murderous covetousness. You will also see the greatest examples of love and sacrifice that mankind has ever contributed. For indeed the Bible is the story of man. It is the whole story, and nothing is left out or omitted. It is the ultimate mirror of life.

When we invest time in the Bible we indulge a bit of the eternal. The Bible will never pass away, even in the eons of the future. If you have read it sincerely then my hope is this small work will intensify your understanding and enjoyment a little more. It is the grandest journey we can make while in this life. Thank you for sharing a portion of your life journey with me.

Kenneth Bow

Introduction to Jeremiah

Which fourteen-year-old boy in your church can you envision preaching and being God's Mouthpiece? That was the age Jeremiah began his prophetic work. He then proceeded to speak to a nation who would not listen for the next 40 years.

He has been called the "weeping prophet" because of the times in his book he sheds tears. Jeremiah prophesied while his nation tottered on the brink of captivity.

Jeremiah certainly lived one of the most dramatic lives in the Bible. It appears he never learned to like his role. He was reluctant and unhappy with the job God asked him to do.

God chose him before he was even born, while he was still in his mother's womb. His assignment was to be over nations, to root out, to tear down, to build and to plant. The only resource he had to accomplish this task was his mouth. His response? "Ah Lord God, I cannot speak, for I am a child" (1.6)

He was given the unusual directive that he could never marry, never attend a happy event or a sad event. He was not to experience any human emotion so he would never be confused as to what he felt. He felt what God felt.

For forty years Jeremiah gave the nation's leaders messages they did not want to hear. They arrested him, they imprisoned him, and they almost killed him. Jeremiah hung on. He let them know that the Babylonians were coming and would carry them into captivity. He warned them that alliances with powers like Egypt would not do any good. They ignored him and he pressed on anyway. Jeremiah made it clear, Judah's only hope was to renew their relationship with the living God.

Jeremiah does not impress us like Isaiah. His book is not poetic or beautiful in imagery. The power of the book comes entirely from the insight of this prophet's mind. He was living a nightmare and that nightmare was coming true. The nation was going under.

No person in the Bible shows their feelings like Jeremiah. He quarreled with God. He told God he wished he were dead. He accused God of being unreliable. And yet, he stood, never wavering. No relationship in the Bible speaks more of what it means to serve God. He continued to follow God no matter what.

He must have tired of the ridicule. He continued to stand alone against the crowd. He spoke dark things in dark times. His message was not wanted or popular. In the end his message proved true. He stands greater and more important to the kingdom of God than the very kings who detested him.

The book of Jeremiah is an anthology of prophecies given at different times. It jumps back and forth and is not in any chronological order. It is a glimpse into the troubled mind of a man trying to warn a drowning nation.

300 years before the nation had been split into two nations with the civil war. Israel and Judah had existed side by side for 200 years. Then, 100 years before, the northern nation had been carried away into captivity into Assyria never to be heard from again. He was seeing deja vu for Judah. This time mighty Babylon was breathing down their neck and invasion was imminent.

Points for Jeremiah:

- Prophesied during 5 kings
- Lived through the Babylonian invasion
- Contemporaries were Zephaniah and Habakkuk
- He was forbidden to marry
- He was forbidden to go to any social meetings, happy or sad
- His book has no particular order
- He was called at 14 years old and preached for 40 years
- Tradition says he was stoned in Egypt at the end of his life
- He was the first person to speak of 70 years, then Daniel wrote of it
- Never liked his role but he obeyed
- His only weapon was his voice
- He was one man against a surging mass going in the opposite direction
- He quarreled with God and told God he wished he were dead (20.14-18)
- Accused God of being unreliable (15.18)
- Had no social life (16.8)

Some of his memorable messages:

- Broken cisterns
- Potters house (18)
- Rechabites (35)
- The miry clay
- The buried sash
- The smashed pot
- Purchasing land for the return after the exile

His supreme contribution:

Jeremiah gives us the high point of the Old Testament. In chapter 31 he gives the turning point after 1000 years of failure as a nation.

God wrote the law on tables of stone and the nation never was able to fulfill their destiny. It was smoke, ashes, debris, and failure. It was time for the second edition to be written.

Abraham was called in 1921 BC. The children of Israel entered Canaan in 1451 BC. It had been 1300 years since Abraham's call and 800 years since they crossed the Jordan. The judges, the kings, the prophets, had all proved unable to stem the downward drift of the nation.

God called a fourteen-year-old boy. God quarantined him from social events, and gave him the New Covenant. 1000 years of history flowed into this young boy's heart. From that river flowed out the New Covenant that is the foundation of the New Testament.

This time God would write it not on tables of stone, but on

their hearts. Jeremiah chapter 31 becomes the foundation of all the teachings of Jesus and the Apostle Paul.

It is an incredible story of an incredible man, used by God.

Author: Jeremiah

Chronology: 629 BC

Jesus in the book: In Matthew 16 Jesus was likened to Jeremiah.

Apostolic Themes: The New Covenant

Chapter 1

1.1-3 The words of Jeremiah the son of Hilkiah, of the priests that were in Anathoth in the land of Benjamin: 2 To whom the word of the Lord came in the days of Josiah the son of Amon king of Judah, in the thirteenth year of his reign. 3 It came also in the days of Jehoiakim the son of Josiah king of Judah, unto the end of the eleventh year of Zedekiah the son of Josiah king of Judah, unto the carrying away of Jerusalem captive in the fifth month.

1.1-3 This opening gives us Jeremiah's pedigree, location, and beginning point. Jeremiah was 14 years old when he began his prophetic career in the 13th year of Josiah's reign. Jeremiah is a major prophet for several reasons. The scope of his work is wide and inclusive. The duration of his work; 40 years. His writings spanned 5 kings and lasted until the Babylonian captivity.

1.4-19 Then the word of the Lord came unto me, saying, 5 Before I formed thee in the belly I knew thee; and before thou camest forth out of the womb I sanctified thee, and I ordained thee a prophet unto the nations. 6 Then said I, Ah, Lord God! behold, I cannot speak: for I am a child. 7 But the Lord said unto me, Say not, I am a child: for thou shalt go to all that I shall send thee, and

whatsoever I command thee thou shalt speak. 8 Be not afraid of their faces: for I am with thee to deliver thee, saith the Lord. 9 Then the Lord put forth his hand, and touched my mouth. And the Lord said unto me, Behold, I have put my words in thy mouth. 10 See, I have this day set thee over the nations and over the kingdoms, to root out, and to pull down, and to destroy, and to throw down, to build, and to plant. 11 Moreover the word of the Lord came unto me, saying, Jeremiah, what seest thou? And I said, I see a rod of an almond tree. 12 Then said the Lord unto me, Thou hast well seen: for I will hasten my word to perform it. 13 And the word of the Lord came unto me the second time, saying, What seest thou? And I said, I see a seething pot; and the face thereof is toward the north. 14 Then the Lord said unto me, Out of the north an evil shall break forth upon all the inhabitants of the land. 15 For, lo, I will call all the families of the kingdoms of the north, saith the Lord; and they shall come, and they shall set every one his throne at the entering of the gates of Jerusalem, and against all the walls thereof round about, and against all the cities of Judah. 16 And I will utter my judgments against them touching all their wickedness, who have forsaken me, and have burned incense unto other gods, and worshipped the works of their own hands. 17 Thou therefore gird up thy loins, and arise, and speak unto them all that I command thee: be not dismayed at their faces, lest I confound thee before them. 18 For, behold, I have made thee this day a defenced city, and an iron pillar, and brasen walls against the whole land, against the kings of Judah, against the princes thereof, against the priests thereof, and against the people of the land. 19 And they shall fight against thee; but they shall not prevail against thee; for I am with thee, saith the Lord, to deliver thee.

1.4-19 His call. There are many unique things about this book of prophecy and one of them is the authorization of the call on his life. He takes time to detail the call from God and it's beginning before he was born. At the outset we see his personality. Jeremiah shows us his arguments with God. Throughout his life, this will surface on occasion. Jeremiah fulfilled his call, but he was quick to vocalize his opinion when he differed with God. In this regard he is one of a kind in the Bible. God responds to Jeremiah's honesty with his own honesty. The road will not be an easy road. The challenge for this young prophet is immense. God gives him two assurances. First the almond tree symbol. The almond tree blooms before any tree in early January, an apt image of the young prophet. The second was a simmering pot. This spoke of the coming judgment from the north that was about to descend on the nation. Jeremiah is to announce these coming judgments. God will embolden him and make him as an iron pillar or a brazen wall. His voice is the voice of God to kings, princes, priests, and people. It will be a lifelong battle for the young prophet. At the outset God assures him his life will be successful.

Chapter 2

2.1-13 Moreover the word of the Lord came to me, saying, 2 Go and cry in the ears of Jerusalem, saying, Thus saith the Lord; I remember thee, the kindness of thy youth, the love of thine espousals, when thou wentest after me in the wilderness, in a land that was not sown. 3 Israel was holiness unto the Lord, and the firstfruits of his increase: all that devour him shall offend; evil shall come upon them, saith the Lord. 4 Hear ye the word of the Lord, O house of Jacob, and all the families of the house of Israel: 5 Thus saith the Lord, What iniquity have your fathers found in me, that they are gone far from me, and have walked after vanity, and are become vain? 6 Neither said they, Where is the Lord that brought us up out of the land of Egypt, that led us through the wilderness, through a land of deserts and of pits, through a land of drought, and of the shadow of death, through a land that no man passed through, and where no man dwelt? 7 And I brought you into a plentiful country, to eat the fruit thereof and the goodness thereof; but when ye entered, ye defiled my land, and made mine heritage an abomination. 8 The priests said not, Where is the Lord? and they that handle the law knew me not: the pastors also transgressed against me, and the prophets prophesied by Baal, and walked after things that do not profit. 9 Wherefore I will yet plead with you, saith the Lord, and with your children's children will I plead. 10 For pass over the isles of Chittim, and see; and send unto Kedar, and consider diligently, and see if there be such a thing. 11 Hath a nation changed their gods, which are yet no gods? but my people have changed their glory for that which doth not profit. 12 Be astonished, O ye heavens, at this, and be horribly afraid, be ye very desolate, saith the Lord. 13 For my people have committed two evils; they have forsaken me the fountain of living waters, and hewed them out cisterns, broken cisterns, that can hold no water.

2.1-13 The appeal. God begins to document his case with the wayward nation. God begins at the moment of tenderness when Israel was young. It was in the early years of the wilderness wandering that Israel went after God. Time has produced a patina of indifference on the relationship. God defends His righteousness toward Israel. He delivered them into the land He promised. The turn began when the spiritual leaders failed in their responsibilities. Priests, prophets and pastors alike all failed in their leadership. The young prophet offers one of his most lasting images of a nation spiraling out of control. He speaks of two evils. They have forsaken the living water and hewn them out cisterns, broken cisterns. Without water every living substance dies. This graphic image is the death signal of the nation.

2.14-37 Is Israel a servant? is he a homeborn slave? why is he spoiled? 15 The young lions roared upon him, and yelled, and they made his land waste: his cities are burned without inhabitant. 16 Also the children of Noph and Tahapanes have broken the crown of thy head. 17 Hast thou not procured this unto thyself, in that thou hast forsaken the Lord thy God, when he led thee by the way? 18 And now what hast thou to do in the way of Egypt, to drink the waters of Sihor? or what hast thou to do in the way of Assyria, to drink the waters of the river? 19 Thine own wickedness shall correct thee, and thy backslidings shall reprove thee: know therefore and see that it is an evil thing and bitter, that thou hast forsaken the Lord thy God, and that my fear is not in thee, saith the Lord God of hosts. 20 For of old time I have broken thy yoke, and burst thy bands; and thou saidst, I will not transgress; when upon every high hill and under every green tree thou wanderest, playing the harlot. 21 Yet I had planted thee a noble vine, wholly a right seed: how then art thou turned into the degenerate plant of a strange vine unto me? 22 For though thou wash thee with nitre, and take thee much soap, yet thine iniquity is marked before me, saith the Lord God. 23 How canst thou say, I am not polluted, I have not gone after Baalim? see thy way in the valley, know what thou hast done: thou art a swift dromedary traversing her ways; 24 A wild ass used to the wilderness, that snuffeth up the wind at her pleasure; in her occasion who can turn her away? all they that seek her will not weary themselves; in her month they shall find her. 25 Withhold thy foot from being unshod, and thy throat from thirst: but thou saidst, There is no hope: no; for I have loved strangers, and after them will I go. 26 As the thief is ashamed when he is found, so is the house of Israel ashamed; they, their kings, their princes, and their priests, and their prophets. 27 Saying to a stock, Thou art my father; and to a stone, Thou hast brought me forth: for they have turned their back unto me, and not their face: but in the time of their trouble they will say, Arise, and save us. 28 But where are thy gods that thou hast made thee? let them arise, if they can save thee in the time of thy trouble: for according to the number of thy cities are thy gods, O Judah. 29 Wherefore will ye plead with me? ye all have transgressed against me, saith the Lord. 30 In vain have I smitten your children; they received no correction: your own sword hath devoured your prophets, like a destroying lion. 31 O generation, see ye the word of the Lord. Have I been a wilderness unto Israel? a land of darkness? wherefore say my people, We are lords; we will come no more unto thee? 32 Can a maid forget her ornaments, or a bride her attire? yet my people have forgotten me days without number. 33 Why trimmest thou thy way to seek love? therefore hast thou also taught the wicked ones thy ways. 34 Also in thy skirts is found the blood of the souls of the poor innocents: I have not found it by secret search, but upon all these. 35 Yet thou sayest, Because I am innocent, surely his anger shall turn from me. Behold, I will plead with thee, because thou sayest, I have not sinned. 36 Why gaddest thou about so much to change thy way? thou also shalt be ashamed of Egypt, as thou wast ashamed of Assyria. 37 Yea, thou shalt go forth from him, and thine hands upon thine head: for the Lord hath rejected thy confidences, and thou shalt not prosper in them.

2.14-37 The argument. God in his own wisdom presents his argument. He has no cause to do this of course. It shows His love for the nation. They have forsaken His living water and drank the waters of Egypt and Assyria. God is documenting their wickedness and placing the upcoming consequences squarely where they belong. God planted them a noble vine and the vine has deteriorated. God lays the abundance of evidence so completely, Israel is without defense. The gods she has sought have been empty and futile. Through all of this incredible slide, Israel maintained her innocence. She is proud and defiant. She boldly declares I have not sinned. Israel changed her gods, acted like a wild ass sniffing every pagan wind, and forgot God. Having laid his evidence down, God now proceeds to the consequences of their unfaithfulness.

Chapter 3

3.1-5 They say, If a man put away his wife, and she go from him, and become another man's, shall he return unto her again? shall not that land be greatly polluted? but thou hast played the harlot with many lovers; yet return again to me, saith the Lord. 2 Lift up thine eyes unto the high places, and see where thou hast not been lien with. In the ways hast thou sat for them, as the Arabian in the wilderness; and thou hast polluted the land with thy whoredoms and with thy wickedness. 3 Therefore the showers have been withholden, and there hath been no latter rain; and thou hadst a whore's forehead, thou refusedst to be ashamed. 4 Wilt thou not from this time cry unto me, My father, thou art the guide of my youth? 5 Will he reserve his anger for ever? will he keep it to the end? Behold, thou hast spoken and done evil things as thou couldest.

3.1-5 Divorce. God opens up the discussion of his disappointment with Judah in a way they can easily relate to. Few, if any people, would not be able to grasp the simple idea of unfaithfulness when presented in the light of divorce. God likens the people of Judah to an unfaithful wife who has been divorced. The departing husband no longer is expected to support the unfaithful wife. She has forfeited her benefits. So God, the faithful husband is withholding the benefits of rain in hopes of wooing back his wife.

3.6-7 The Lord said also unto me in the days of Josiah the king, Hast thou seen that which backsliding Israel hath done? she is gone up upon every high mountain and under every green tree, and there hath played the harlot. 7 And I said after she had done all these things, Turn thou unto me. But she returned not. And her treacherous sister Judah saw it.

3.6-7 Judah is not inclined to listen. She continues on in her pseudo religion and false faith. Judah seeks the gods of the nations around her and does not return to her faithful husband. Having taken this posture, God now must judge her and here begins the first of four sermons predicting Judah's coming judgment. The remainder of this chapter and into chapter 4.4 is the first message of judgment. These messages continue through chapter 6.

3.8-25 And I saw, when for all the causes whereby backsliding Israel committed adultery I had put her away, and given her a bill of divorce; yet her treacherous sister Judah feared not, but went and played the harlot also. 9 And it came to pass through the lightness of her whoredom, that she defiled the land, and committed adultery with stones and with stocks. 10 And yet for all this her treacherous sister Judah hath not turned unto me with her whole heart, but feignedly, saith the Lord. 11 And the Lord said unto me, The backsliding Israel hath justified herself more than treacherous Judah. 12 Go and proclaim these words toward the north, and say, Return, thou backsliding Israel, saith the Lord; and I will not cause mine anger to fall upon you: for I am

merciful, saith the Lord, and I will not keep anger for ever. 13 Only acknowledge thine iniquity, that thou hast transgressed against the Lord thy God, and hast scattered thy ways to the strangers under every green tree, and ye have not obeyed my voice, saith the Lord. 14 Turn, O backsliding children, saith the Lord; for I am married unto you: and I will take you one of a city, and two of a family, and I will bring you to Zion: 15 And I will give you pastors according to mine heart, which shall feed you with knowledge and understanding. 16 And it shall come to pass, when ye be multiplied and increased in the land, in those days, saith the Lord, they shall say no more, The ark of the covenant of the Lord: neither shall it come to mind: neither shall they remember it; neither shall they visit it; neither shall that be done any more. 17 At that time they shall call Jerusalem the throne of the Lord; and all the nations shall be gathered unto it, to the name of the Lord, to Jerusalem: neither shall they walk any more after the imagination of their evil heart. 18 In those days the house of Judah shall walk with the house of Israel, and they shall come together out of the land of the north to the land that I have given for an inheritance unto your fathers. 19 But I said, How shall I put thee among the children, and give thee a pleasant land, a goodly heritage of the hosts of nations? and I said, Thou shalt call me, My father; and shalt not turn away from me. 20 Surely as a wife treacherously departeth from her husband, so have ye dealt treacherously with me, O house of Israel, saith the Lord. 21 A voice was heard upon the high places, weeping and supplications of the children of Israel: for they have perverted their way, and they have forgotten the Lord their God. 22 Return, ye backsliding children, and I will heal your backslidings. Behold, we come unto thee; for thou art the Lord our God. 23 Truly in vain is salvation hoped for from the

hills, and from the multitude of mountains: truly in the Lord our God is the salvation of Israel. 24 For shame hath devoured the labour of our fathers from our youth; their flocks and their herds, their sons and their daughters. 25 We lie down in our shame, and our confusion covereth us: for we have sinned against the Lord our God, we and our fathers, from our youth even unto this day, and have not obeyed the voice of the Lord our God.

3.8-25 Backsliding. Many of the ideologies of the Old Testament are not incorporated into the reality of New Testament daily life. In this case this idea of backsliding is very much a part of the New Covenant theology. It is at the root of the message of Jeremiah and will be the hub of the New Testament church doctrine. This is seen in the parables of Jesus, the ministry of Paul the Apostle, and particularly in the Book of Hebrews. Backsliding is a term in Hebrew (meshubah), that means apostasy or turning away. It carries the connotation of going back to the former ways. It always involves wanting to do things our way rather than the way God has instructed. It involves turning away from the salvation provided by God and seeking other means to be saved, delivered, or fulfilled. God shows his long suffering and is magnanimous in His mercy toward this nation. The answer God provides to stop this hemorrhage of faith is that He will give them pastors, (15). The meaning here is a shepherd. This concept and solution is also continued in the New Testament. God provides a shepherd under Himself and calls this office the under shepherd (1 Pet 5.1-4). This is also developed into a doctrine in Eph 4.11. A pastor is a shepherd. This is the solution given by God to combat backsliding. For this reason there is always intense spiritual warfare against the ministry of a pastor for he is the primary defense against people returning to their old life of idolatry. The ark, which symbolized the presence of God, is now to be replaced with God himself being present among them. The prophecy gives hope of future restoration with the northern nation that has been extinct for 100 years. This message closes with the return to the refrain of the treacherous wife. The jilted husband weeps and laments, return ye backsliding children. The echo of that passionate cry is still on the air today and calls to every wayward child of God, return and be saved.

Chapter 4

4.1-4 If thou wilt return, O Israel, saith the Lord, return unto me: and if thou wilt put away thine abominations out of my sight, then shalt thou not remove. 2 And thou shalt swear, The Lord liveth, in truth, in judgment, and in righteousness; and the nations shall bless themselves in him, and in him shall they glory. 3 For thus saith the Lord to the men of Judah and Jerusalem, Break up your fallow ground, and sow not among thorns. 4 Circumcise yourselves to the Lord, and take away the foreskins of your heart, ye men of Judah and inhabitants of Jerusalem: lest my fury come forth like fire, and burn that none can quench it, because of the evil of your doings.

4.1-4 This is the conclusion of the message in chapter three. Jeremiah introduces in these verses what will eventually become his most prominent theme of his prophecy. God no longer is looking to find people who live for Him out of obligation to rules. God is going to introduce the grand idea of a New Covenant. In this New Covenant God will seek to write His laws on men's hearts, not on tables of stone. This is a revolutionary concept that Jesus will pick up and preach, and Paul the Apostle will refine in his 14 epistles. This is very possibly the greatest revelation and message of the entire Old Testament. It is the basis for all New Testament doctrine and theology.

4.5-18 Declare ye in Judah, and publish in Jerusalem; and say, Blow ye the trumpet in the land: cry, gather together, and say, Assemble yourselves, and let us go into the defenced cities. 6 Set up the standard toward Zion: retire, stay not: for I will bring evil from the north, and a great destruction. 7 The lion is come up from his thicket, and the destroyer of the Gentiles is on his way; he is gone forth from his place to make thy land desolate; and thy cities shall be laid waste, without an inhabitant. 8 For this gird you with sackcloth, lament and howl: for the fierce anger of the Lord is not turned back from us. 9 And it shall come to pass at that day, saith the Lord, that the heart of the king shall perish, and the heart of the princes; and the priests shall be astonished, and the prophets shall wonder. 10 Then said I, Ah, Lord God! surely thou hast greatly deceived this people and Jerusalem, saying, Ye shall have peace; whereas the sword reacheth unto the soul. 11 At that time shall it be said to this people and to Jerusalem, A dry wind of the high places in the wilderness toward the daughter of my people, not to fan, nor to cleanse, 12 Even a full wind from those places shall come unto me: now also will I give sentence against them. 13 Behold, he shall come up as clouds, and his chariots shall be as a whirlwind: his horses are swifter than eagles. Woe unto us! for we are spoiled. 14 O Jerusalem, wash thine heart from wickedness, that thou mayest be saved. How long shall thy vain thoughts lodge within thee? 15 For a voice declareth from Dan, and publisheth affliction from mount Ephraim. 16 Make ye mention to the nations; behold, publish against Jerusalem, that watchers come from a far country, and give out their voice against the cities of Judah. 17 As keepers of a field, are they against her round about; because she hath been rebellious against me, saith the Lord. 18 Thy way and thy doings have procured these things unto thee; this is thy wickedness, because it is bitter, because it reacheth unto thine heart.

4.5-18 The lion in the thicket. Jeremiah lifts his voice like a trumpet; there is danger coming. This is ever the purpose of the ministry. All the populace, including Jeremiah, were expecting peace. God reveals, this is not to be so. The lion is crouched and watching from the thicket. The lion will pounce. Later in chapter 50.17 Jeremiah identifies the lion as Nebuchadnezzar, King of Babylon. Sounding the warning like a trumpet, Jeremiah warns the lion is stalking and watching from the thicket. The jilted, discarded husband will not protect the unfaithful wife against the lion in the thicket.

4.19-31 My bowels, my bowels! I am pained at my very heart; my heart maketh a noise in me; I cannot hold my peace, because thou hast heard, O my soul, the sound of the trumpet, the alarm of war. 20 Destruction upon destruction is cried; for the whole land is spoiled: suddenly are my tents spoiled, and my curtains in a moment. 21 How long shall I see the standard, and hear the sound of the trumpet? 22 For my people is foolish, they have not known me; they are sottish children, and they have none understanding: they are wise to do evil, but to do good they have no knowledge. 23 I beheld the earth, and, lo, it was without form, and void; and the heavens, and they had no light. 24 I beheld the mountains, and, lo, they trembled, and all the hills moved lightly. 25 I beheld, and, lo, there was no man, and all the birds of the heavens were fled. 26 I beheld, and, lo, the fruitful place was a wilderness, and all the cities thereof were broken down at the presence of the Lord, and by his fierce anger. 27 For thus hath the Lord said, The whole land shall be desolate; yet will I not make a full end. 28 For this shall the earth mourn, and the heavens above be black; because I have spoken it, I have purposed it, and will not repent, neither will I turn back from it. 29 The whole city shall flee for the noise of the horsemen and bowmen; they shall go into thickets, and climb up upon the rocks: every city shall be forsaken, and not a man dwell therein. 30 And when thou art spoiled, what wilt thou do? Though thou clothest thyself with crimson, though thou deckest thee with ornaments of gold, though thou rentest thy face with painting, in vain shalt thou make thyself fair; thy lovers will despise thee, they will seek thy life. 31 For I have heard a voice as of a woman in travail, and the anguish as of her that bringeth forth her first child, the voice of the daughter of Zion, that bewaileth herself, that spreadeth her hands, saying, Woe is me now! for my soul is wearied because of murderers.

4.19-31 The anguish of the prophet. This insight is helpful to understand the inner feelings of men called of God to deliver God's word. Many times the man is sad or even sick with what he is told to speak. He knows the people will think it is his own attitude bleeding through. Here we see a classic example of this conundrum every man deals with who speaks for God. Jeremiah is sick inside. His heart hurts. The voice inside of him cannot be silenced. The voice is screaming inside his head. Men who speak for God are a unique breed. They must divest themselves of personal opinion and motive. They are to be a conduit from the mouth of God to the people. In addition to this, they must ignore their own feelings and inclinations. This is far from easy to do as we see here in the dilemma Jeremiah faces in delivering this message to the people he loves. He is instructed to proclaim the coming horrors that will befall this nation. He faithfully does as he is commanded. With passion and vivid detail, he announces the coming desolation, which is destruction so complete as to cause astonishment. Over the din of battle and wails of death, Jeremiah can hear the voice of a woman in travail as her anguish gushes out of her inner being. Horror stricken beyond words, she simply moans, "woe is me". The coming destruction by the Lion in the thicket is so terrible as to be beyond words. With graphic detail and words of horror, the young prophet is speaking the heart of God for his unfaithful wife to return to Him. Her response is forth coming in chapter 5. This ends the second message of Jeremiah.

Chapter 5

5.1-10 Run ye to and fro through the streets of Jerusalem, and see now, and know, and seek in the broad places thereof, if ye can find a man, if there be any that executeth judgment, that seeketh the truth; and I will pardon it. 2 And though they say, The Lord liveth; surely they swear falsely. 3 O Lord, are not thine eyes upon the truth? thou hast stricken them, but they have not grieved; thou hast consumed them, but they have refused to receive correction: they have made their faces harder than a rock; they have refused to return. 4 Therefore I said, Surely these are poor; they are foolish: for they know not the way of the Lord, nor the judgment of their God. 5 I will get me unto the great men, and will speak unto them; for they have known the way of the Lord, and the judgment of their God: but these have altogether broken the yoke, and burst the bonds. 6 Wherefore a lion out of the forest shall slay them, and a wolf of the evenings shall spoil them, a leopard shall watch over their cities: every one that goeth out thence shall be torn in pieces: because their transgressions are many, and their backslidings are increased. 7 How shall I pardon thee for this? thy children have forsaken me, and sworn by them that are no gods: when I had fed them to the full, they then committed adultery, and assembled themselves by troops in the harlots' houses. 8 They were as fed horses in the morning: every one neighed after his neighbour's wife. 9 Shall I not visit for these things? saith the Lord: and shall not my soul be avenged on such a nation as this? 10 Go ye up upon her walls, and destroy; but make not a full end: take away her battlements; for they are not the Lord's.

5.1-10 When God destroyed Sodom He promised He would spare the city if there were 10 righteous people there. Here God is only looking for one. This is to illustrate how great the sin of Judah was. The eyes of the Lord have seen Judah's sin. A lion out of the forest is waiting to slay them. They have desired their neighbor's wife, and God will visit (bring chastisement) them.

5.11-13 For the house of Israel and the house of Judah have dealt very treacherously against me, saith the Lord. 12 They have belied the Lord, and said, It is not he; neither shall evil come upon us; neither shall we see sword nor famine: 13 And the prophets shall become wind, and the word is not in them: thus shall it be done unto them.

5.11-13 False prophets. To add to the sin and coming judgment, there were false prophets among the people. This added to the people's sense of comfort and complacency. There are few things more damaging to the work of God. The image here in relation to the wind speaks of windbags. This is how God sees these prophets. These prophets are not sent by God, they are deceitful.

5.14-31 Wherefore thus saith the Lord God of hosts, Because ye speak this word, behold, I will make my words in thy mouth fire, and this people wood, and it

shall devour them. 15 Lo, I will bring a nation upon you from far, O house of Israel, saith the Lord: it is a mighty nation, it is an ancient nation, a nation whose language thou knowest not, neither understandest what they say. 16 Their quiver is as an open sepulchre, they are all mighty men. 17 And they shall eat up thine harvest, and thy bread, which thy sons and thy daughters should eat: they shall eat up thy flocks and thine herds: they shall eat up thy vines and thy fig trees: they shall impoverish thy fenced cities, wherein thou trustedst, with the sword. 18 Nevertheless in those days, saith the Lord, I will not make a full end with you. 19 And it shall come to pass, when ye shall say, Wherefore doeth the Lord our God all these things unto us? then shalt thou answer them, Like as ye have forsaken me, and served strange gods in your land, so shall ye serve strangers in a land that is not your's. 20 Declare this in the house of Jacob, and publish it in Judah, saying, 21 Hear now this, O foolish people, and without understanding; which have eyes, and see not; which have ears, and hear not: 22 Fear ye not me? saith the Lord: will ye not tremble at my presence, which have placed the sand for the bound of the sea by a perpetual decree, that it cannot pass it: and though the waves thereof toss themselves, yet can they not prevail; though they roar, yet can they not pass over it? 23 But this people hath a revolting and a rebellious heart; they are revolted and gone. 24 Neither say they in their heart, Let us now fear the Lord our God, that giveth rain, both the former and the latter, in his season: he reserveth unto us the appointed weeks of the harvest. 25 Your iniquities have turned away these things, and your sins have withholden good things from you. 26 For among my people are found wicked men: they lay wait, as he that setteth snares; they set a trap, they catch men. 27 As a cage is full of birds, so are their houses full of deceit:

therefore they are become great, and waxen rich. 28 They are waxen fat, they shine: yea, they overpass the deeds of the wicked: they judge not the cause, the cause of the fatherless, yet they prosper; and the right of the needy do they not judge. 29 Shall I not visit for these things? saith the Lord: shall not my soul be avenged on such a nation as this? 30 A wonderful and horrible thing is committed in the land; 31 The prophets prophesy falsely, and the priests bear rule by their means; and my people love to have it so: and what will ye do in the end thereof?

5.14-31 The snares. God remembers. When it is good God remembers. When it is bad God also remembers. God remembered the covenant on Sinai, and now he keeps his promise. In Deut. 29.24-26 this was promised if the people of God forsook Him. To fulfill this, God allows men to set snares among His people. These people have lost their fear of God. The iniquities (to twist or pervert) they have succumbed to, have kept the blessings of God away from them in the harvest season. The houses of these people are full of deceit. They have lost all sense of moral judgment. The false prophets deceive the people and the people love to have it so. This is wonderful (astonishing) and horrible (fearful). God has more to say.

Chapter 6

6.1-8 O ye children of Benjamin, gather yourselves to flee out of the midst of Jerusalem, and blow the trumpet in Tekoa, and set up a sign of fire in Bethhaccerem: for evil appeareth out of the north, and great destruction. 2 I have likened the daughter of Zion to a comely and delicate woman. 3 The shepherds with their flocks shall come unto her; they shall pitch their tents against her round about; they shall feed every one in his place. 4 Prepare ye war against her; arise, and let us go up at noon. Woe unto us! for the day goeth away, for the shadows of the evening are stretched out. 5 Arise, and let us go by night, and let us destroy her palaces. 6 For thus hath the Lord of hosts said, Hew ye down trees, and cast a mount against Jerusalem: this is the city to be visited; she is wholly oppression in the midst of her. 7 As a fountain casteth out her waters, so she casteth out her wickedness: violence and spoil is heard in her; before me continually is grief and wounds. 8 Be thou instructed, O Jerusalem, lest my soul depart from thee; lest I make thee desolate, a land not inhabited.

6.1-8 Impending disaster. 5 times in this chapter it says thus hath the Lord of hosts said. In the opening verses a signal fire is mentioned. This announces an emergency, along with the blowing of trumpets. The first of the times God speaks is about a mount against Jerusalem. There will be a siege.

6.9-15 Thus saith the Lord of hosts, They shall throughly glean the remnant of Israel as a vine: turn back thine hand as a grapegatherer into the baskets. 10 To whom shall I speak, and give warning, that they may hear? behold, their ear is uncircumcised, and they cannot hearken: behold, the word of the Lord is unto them a reproach; they have no delight in it. 11 Therefore I am full of the fury of the Lord; I am weary with holding in: I will pour it out upon the children abroad, and upon the assembly of young men together: for even the husband with the wife shall be taken, the aged with him that is full of days. 12 And their houses shall be turned unto others, with their fields and wives together: for I will stretch out my hand upon the inhabitants of the land, saith the Lord. 13 For from the least of them even unto the greatest of them every one is given to covetousness; and from the prophet even unto the priest every one dealeth falsely. 14 They have healed also the hurt of the daughter of my people slightly, saying, Peace, peace; when there is no peace. 15 Were they ashamed when they had committed abomination? nay, they were not at all ashamed, neither could they blush: therefore they shall fall among them that fall: at the time that I visit them they shall be cast down, saith the Lord.

6.9-15 The second word. The coming destruction is likened to a gleaning in the field. There is an interlude here where we see Jeremiah sad about what is coming. The prophet's compassion is revealed toward the nation he loved. The hand of God is still outstretched, a symbol of mercy. This is an offering from God because the prophets have prophesied peace, when there will be no peace. The concept of peace, in relation to no war, was not the primary meaning of peace. True peace is inner. It is attaining personal fulfillment and enjoying healthy relationships. This is accomplished by accepting the Prince of Peace (Jesus Christ) into your life.

6.16-20 Thus saith the Lord, Stand ye in the ways, and see, and ask for the old paths, where is the good way, and walk therein, and ye shall find rest for your souls. But they said, We will not walk therein. 17 Also I set watchmen over you, saying, Hearken to the sound of the trumpet. But they said, We will not hearken. 18 Therefore hear, ye nations, and know, O congregation, what is among them. 19 Hear, O earth: behold, I will bring evil upon this people, even the fruit of their thoughts, because they have not hearkened unto my words, nor to my law, but rejected it. 20 To what purpose cometh there to me incense from Sheba, and the sweet cane from a far country? your burnt offerings are not acceptable, nor your sacrifices sweet unto me.

6.16-20 The third word. The prophet encourages the people to return to the old paths. The watchmen, the trumpets, and the old paths are all a call to return to the lord. The sacrifices offered by these people are unacceptable to God. It is not too late to salvage this nation, but there must be a return to God. The return to the old paths is a timeless theme that has been needed in every generation. The meaning is apropos here and is also apropos to every era.

6.21 Therefore thus saith the Lord, Behold, I will lay stumblingblocks before this people, and the fathers and the sons together shall fall upon them; the neighbour and his friend shall perish.

6.21 The fourth word. God will lay stumbling blocks in their path to slow down the rush to judgment. God's reason for these stumbling blocks is not to harm, but rather in hopes the people might wake up and repent before it is too late. Often Jeremiah is like a man waving his arms and yelling trying to get the people to wake up and see their plight.

6.22-30 Thus saith the Lord, Behold, a people cometh from the north country, and a great nation shall be raised from the sides of the earth. 23 They shall lay hold on bow and spear; they are cruel, and have no mercy; their voice roareth like the sea; and they ride upon horses, set in array as men for war against thee, O daughter of Zion. 24 We have heard the fame thereof: our hands wax feeble: anguish hath taken hold of us, and pain, as of a woman in travail. 25 Go not forth into the field, nor walk by the way; for the sword of the enemy and fear is on every side. 26 O daughter of my people, gird thee with sackcloth, and wallow thyself in ashes: make thee mourning, as for an only son, most bitter lamentation: for the spoiler shall suddenly come upon us. 27 I have set thee for a tower and a fortress among my people, that thou mayest know and try their way. 28 They are all grievous revolters, walking with slanders: they are brass and iron; they are all corrupters. 29 The bellows are burned, the lead is consumed of the fire; the founder melteth in vain: for the wicked are not plucked away. 30 Reprobate silver shall men call them, because the Lord hath rejected them.

6.22-30 The fifth word. Judgment is on its way. Why? Because the people have been reprobate silver. The bellows are burned, the lead is consumed, and still the impurities are not removed. The analogy is to silver being refined. The fire is so hot it destroys everything, and the impurity is still there. So are these people. God has sent every form of judgment and destruction and still the sin is not removed. They are reprobate silver in God's hand. The fire of His judgment is so hot it will consume everything and the impurities will never be removed. The lion in the thicket is crouched and waiting, Babylon is coming.

Chapter 7

7.1-2 The word that came to Jeremiah from the Lord, saying, 2 Stand in the gate of the Lord's house, and proclaim there this word, and say, Hear the word of the Lord, all ye of Judah, that enter in at these gates to worship the Lord.

7.1-2 The Temple Gate message. Chapters 7-10 are called the Temple Gate message. These chapters reveal the causes of Judah's judgment. It takes a while to log all her many transgressions. This wayward nation has long been chasing the idols of the nations around her.

7.3-11 Thus saith the Lord of hosts, the God of Israel, Amend your ways and your doings, and I will cause you to dwell in this place. 4 Trust ye not in lying words, saying, The temple of the Lord, The temple of the Lord, The temple of the Lord, are these. 5 For if ye throughly amend your ways and your doings; if ye throughly execute judgment between a man and his neighbour; 6 If ye oppress not the stranger, the fatherless, and the widow, and shed not innocent blood in this place, neither walk after other gods to your hurt: 7 Then will I cause you to dwell in this place, in the land that I gave to your fathers, for ever and ever. 8 Behold, ye trust in lying

words, that cannot profit. 9 Will ye steal, murder, and commit adultery, and swear falsely, and burn incense unto Baal, and walk after other gods whom ye know not; 10 And come and stand before me in this house, which is called by my name, and say, We are delivered to do all these abominations? 11 Is this house, which is called by my name, become a den of robbers in your eyes? Behold, even I have seen it, saith the Lord.

7.3-11 Amend your ways. Judah is admonished to amend (make better) her ways. She is at fault for her ways concerning the temple. She has oppressed many people. She has trusted in lying words, committed murder, and served idols. She then came to the temple and boldly acted as though all was well. God says this makes the Temple a den of robbers. Formal attendance to the Temple is condemned. This is also condemned in the New Testament, Mt 21.13. Malachi, the final voice of the Old Testament, speaks of this just before God goes silent for 400 years. Malachi said they had found the table of the Lord contemptible.

7.12-29 But go ye now unto my place which was in Shiloh, where I set my name at the first, and see what I did to it for the wickedness of my people Israel. 13 And now, because ye have done all these works, saith the Lord, and I spake unto you, rising up early and speaking, but ye heard not; and I called you, but ye answered not; 14 Therefore will I do unto this house, which is called by my name, wherein ye trust, and unto the place which I gave to you and to your fathers, as I have done to Shiloh. 15 And I will cast you out of my sight, as I have cast out all your brethren, even the whole seed of Ephraim. 16 Therefore pray not thou for this people, neither lift up cry nor prayer for them, neither make intercession to me: for I will not hear thee. 17 Seest thou not what they do in the cities of Judah and in the streets of Jerusalem? 18 The children gather wood, and the fathers kindle the fire, and the women knead their dough, to make cakes to the queen of heaven, and to pour out drink offerings unto other gods, that they may provoke me to anger. 19 Do they provoke me to anger? saith the Lord: do they not provoke themselves to the confusion of their own faces? 20 Therefore thus saith the Lord God; Behold, mine anger and my fury shall be poured out upon this place, upon man, and upon beast, and upon the trees of the field, and upon the fruit of the ground; and it shall burn, and shall not be quenched. 21 Thus saith the Lord of hosts, the God of Israel; Put your burnt offerings unto your sacrifices, and eat flesh. 22 For I spake not unto your fathers, nor commanded them in the day that I brought them out of the land of Egypt, concerning burnt offerings or sacrifices: 23 But this thing commanded I them, saying, Obey my voice, and I will be your God, and ye shall be my people: and walk ye in all the ways that I have commanded you, that it may be well unto you. 24 But they hearkened not, nor inclined their ear, but walked in the counsels and in the imagination of their evil heart, and went backward, and not forward. 25 Since the day that your fathers came forth out of the land of Egypt unto this day I have even sent unto you all my servants the prophets, daily rising up early and sending them: 26 Yet they hearkened not unto me, nor inclined their ear, but hardened their neck: they did worse than their fathers. 27 Therefore thou shalt speak all these words unto them; but they will not hearken to thee: thou shalt also call unto them; but they will not answer thee. 28 But thou shalt say unto them, This is a nation that obeyeth not the voice of the Lord their God, nor receiveth correction: truth is perished, and is cut off from their mouth. 29 Cut off thine hair, O Jerusalem, and cast it away, and take up a lamentation on high places; for the Lord hath rejected and forsaken the generation of his wrath.

7.12-29 Shiloh. The history of Shiloh testifies how God feels about this kind of travesty. Shiloh was judged by God. God will do the same to this Temple. God instructs Jeremiah to not pray for this people for He will not hear. God has tried since the days of the Exodus from Egypt. God has sent preachers and prophets, but Judah has not listened. God is not telling them to not offer sacrifices; God is telling them the attitude of the believer must be sincere for the sacrifice to have meaning. Jeremiah is instructed to speak unto them but warned they will not hear his words. They had become hard and would not receive correction. Truth was cut off out of their mouth. Judah is told to cut off her hair, a sign of distress.

7.30-34 For the children of Judah have done evil in my sight, saith the Lord: they have set their abominations in the house which is called by my name, to pollute it. 31 And they have built the high places of Tophet, which is in the valley of the son of Hinnom, to burn their sons and their daughters in the fire; which I commanded them not, neither came it into my heart. 32 Therefore, behold, the days come, saith the Lord, that it shall no more be called Tophet, nor the valley of the son of Hinnom, but the valley of slaughter: for they shall bury in Tophet, till there be no place. 33 And the carcases of this people shall be meat for the fowls of the heaven, and for the beasts of the earth; and none shall fray them away. 34 Then will I cause to cease from the cities of Judah, and from the streets of Jerusalem, the voice of mirth, and the voice of gladness, the voice of

the bridegroom, and the voice of the bride: for the land shall be desolate.

7.30-34 Valley of Hinnom. This is the valley on the east side of Jerusalem. It was a place of burning. The refuse of the city was carted there and burned. It became a place of idolatry and also where people offered their children to false gods (Molech) in sacrifice. It became a place where they beat drums continuously to drown out the wails of the mothers whose children were sacrificed. This is the valley Jeremiah says will become the valley of slaughter. Archaeology has confirmed these sacrifices occurred here in this valley. In the shadow of God's chosen city with Solomon's temple nearby, the most horrific idol worship was occurring. God was sick to His stomach of this spiritual adultery.

Chapter 8

8.1-3 At that time, saith the Lord, they shall bring out the bones of the kings of Judah, and the bones of his princes, and the bones of the priests, and the bones of the prophets, and the bones of the inhabitants of Jerusalem, out of their graves: 2 And they shall spread them before the sun, and the moon, and all the host of heaven, whom they have loved, and whom they have served, and after whom they have walked, and whom they have sought, and whom they have worshipped: they shall not be gathered, nor be buried; they shall be for dung upon the face of the earth. 3 And death shall be chosen rather than life by all the residue of them that remain of this evil family, which remain in all the places whither I have driven them, saith the Lord of hosts.

8.1-3 The bones. God now announces he can also burn some things with fire. They were sacrificing their children in fires, so God says I will raise all the bones of all those who have rejected me. Sinners long dead will be laid in the sun and their bones will rot. These sinners' bones will be brought out. This was most likely fulfilled in the invasion of Babylon according to Micah 3.12. Jerusalem was to be plowed like a field.

8.4-12 Moreover thou shalt say unto them, Thus saith the Lord; Shall they fall, and not arise? shall he turn away, and not return? 5 Why then is this people of Jerusalem slidden back by a perpetual backsliding? they hold fast deceit, they refuse to return. 6 I hearkened and heard, but they spake not aright: no man repented him of his wickedness, saying, What have I done? every one turned to his course, as the horse rusheth into the battle. 7 Yea, the stork in the heaven knoweth her appointed times; and the turtle and the crane and the swallow observe the time of their coming; but my people know not the judgment of the Lord. 8 How do ye say, We are wise, and the law of the Lord is with us? Lo, certainly in vain made he it; the pen of the scribes is in vain. 9 The wise men are ashamed, they are dismayed and taken: lo, they have rejected the word of the Lord; and what wisdom is in them? 10 Therefore will I give their wives unto others, and their fields to them that shall inherit them: for every one from the least even unto the greatest is given to covetousness, from the prophet even unto the priest every one dealeth falsely. 11 For they have healed the hurt of the daughter of my people slightly, saying, Peace, peace; when there is no peace. 12 Were they ashamed when they had committed abomination? nay, they were not at all ashamed, neither could they blush: therefore shall they fall among them that fall: in the time of their visitation they shall be cast down, saith the Lord.

8.4-12 Scribes. The people were perpetually backsliding. Even the animals of nature showed more innate understanding than God's people. Even the scribes show misdirected wisdom. These scribes reject commitment to the Word of God. The office of a scribe had been in place for a long time by the time of this writing. Maybe as early as the days of Hezekiah (2K 18.18). These wise men so called were the biggest problem Jeremiah had to deal with. Many times he raises his voice in protest to their false prophecy. These scribes or wise men as they were called were prophesying relief for Judah from suffering when God was turning them over to Babylon for judgment. The lies these men spoke made them the enemies of God. The lies these men spoke were for personal gain, so God takes their lands and their wives and gives all this to others. This seems to have continued for in the days of Jesus the guild of the scribes came under scathing rebuke by Jesus. (Mt 23.13-36).

8.13-17 I will surely consume them, saith the Lord: there shall be no grapes on the vine, nor figs on the fig tree, and the leaf shall fade; and the things that I have given them shall pass away from them. 14 Why do we sit still? assemble yourselves, and let us enter into the defenced cities, and let us be silent there: for the Lord our God hath put us to silence, and given us water of gall to drink, because we have sinned against the Lord. 15 We looked for peace, but no good came; and for a time of health, and behold trouble! 16 The snorting of his horses was heard from Dan: the whole land trembled at the sound of the neighing of his strong ones; for they are come, and have devoured the land, and all that is in it; the city, and those that dwell therein. 17 For, behold, I will send serpents, cockatrices, among you, which will not be charmed, and they shall bite you, saith the Lord.

8.13-17. The very symbol of the covenant God made with Israel was now to be taken away. The fruit of the Promised Land is to be destroyed. The announcement that the trouble is from the north in the direction of Dan is again repeated. The dreadful image of serpents and cockatrices looms.

8.18-22 When I would comfort myself against sorrow, my heart is faint in me. 19 Behold the voice of the cry of the daughter of my people because of them that dwell in a far country: Is not the Lord in Zion? is not her king in her? Why have they provoked me to anger with their graven images, and with strange vanities? 20 The harvest is past, the summer is ended, and we are not saved. 21 For the hurt of the daughter of my people am I hurt; I am black; astonishment hath taken hold on me. 22 Is there no balm in Gilead; is there no physician there? Why then is not the health of the daughter of my people recovered?

8.18-22 The harvest is past. This phrase is one of the most familiar in Jeremiah as well as the rest of the Bible. It is pregnant with imagery. As a farmer has worked the entire season to bring a harvest and at the time of reaping there is no harvest, so God illustrates that is the image here. God has worked for years on this field and no fruit has come. Jeremiah is dismayed and cries out because the sin of the people is incurable. There is no balm in Gilead. The pathos of the prophet bleeds through here and we feel the pain of Jeremiah. He is black with dismay. He is heartbroken and seized by grief. He views the coming judgment as hopeless and inevitable.

Chapter 9

9.1-16 Oh that my head were waters, and mine eyes a fountain of tears, that I might weep day and night for the slain of the daughter of my people! 2 Oh that I had in the wilderness a lodging place of wayfaring men; that I might leave my people, and go from them! for they be all adulterers, an assembly of treacherous men. 3 And they bend their tongues like their bow for lies: but they are not valiant for the truth upon the earth; for they proceed from evil to evil, and they know not me, saith the Lord. 4 Take ye heed every one of his neighbour, and trust ye not in any brother: for every brother will utterly supplant, and every neighbour will walk with slanders. 5 And they will deceive every one his neighbour, and will not speak the truth: they have taught their tongue to speak lies, and weary themselves to commit iniquity. 6 Thine habitation is in the midst of deceit; through deceit they refuse to know me, saith the Lord. 7 Therefore thus saith the Lord of hosts, Behold, I will melt them, and try them; for how shall I do for the daughter of my people? 8 Their tongue is as an arrow shot out; it speaketh deceit: one speaketh peaceably to his neighbour with his mouth, but in heart he layeth his wait. 9 Shall I not visit them for these things? saith the Lord: shall not my soul be avenged on such a nation as this? 10 For the mountains will I take up a weeping and wailing, and for the habitations of the wilderness a lamentation, because they are burned up, so that none can pass through them; neither can men hear the voice of the cattle; both the fowl of the heavens and the beast are fled; they are gone. 11 And I will make Jerusalem heaps, and a den of dragons; and I will make the cities of Judah desolate, without an inhabitant. 12 Who is the wise man, that may understand this? and who is he to whom the mouth of the Lord hath spoken, that he may declare it, for what the land perisheth and is burned up like a wilderness, that none passeth through? 13 And the Lord saith, Because they have forsaken my law which I set before them, and have not obeyed my voice, neither walked therein; 14 But have walked after the imagination of their own heart, and after Baalim, which their fathers taught them: 15 Therefore thus saith the Lord of hosts, the God of Israel; Behold, I will feed them, even this people, with wormwood, and give them water of gall to drink. 16 I will scatter them also among the heathen, whom neither they nor their fathers have known: and I will send a sword after them, till I have consumed them.

9.1-16 Jeremiah the weeping prophet. This is a common feeling among all people. Jeremiah wishes he could just run away. The sadness is too much for him and he feels overwhelmed. Where there was once laughter and joy, now there is bloodshed and death. Weeping seems his only response as words are inadequate. Nature feels the same response as the birds stop singing, the cattle stop lowing, and jackals overrun the ruins of Jerusalem. Jeremiah is to be admired in that he never stood aside like a moralist and became indifferent to others sufferings. He hurt with the people (8.21). Jeremiah felt the bitter judgment he was pronouncing on the nation. In this area he points to another who will come and be labeled a man of sorrows, Jesus Christ himself. In chapter 11.18 Jeremiah even likens himself to a lamb for sacrifice. This again foreshadows Jesus who was the Lamb of God.

9.17-26 Thus saith the Lord of hosts, Consider ye, and call for the mourning women, that they may come; and send for cunning women, that they may come: 18 And let them make haste, and take up a wailing for us, that our eyes may run down with tears, and our eyelids gush out with waters. 19 For a voice of wailing is heard out of Zion, How are we spoiled! we are greatly confounded, because we have forsaken the land, because our dwellings have cast us out. 20 Yet hear the word of the Lord, O ye women, and let your ear receive the word of his mouth, and teach your daughters wailing, and every one her neighbour lamentation. 21 For death is come up into our windows, and is entered into our palaces, to cut off the children from without, and the young men from the streets. 22 Speak, Thus saith the Lord, Even the carcases of men shall fall as dung upon the open field, and as the handful after the harvestman, and none shall gather them. 23 Thus saith the Lord, Let not the wise man glory in his wisdom, neither let the mighty man glory in his might, let not the rich man glory in his riches: 24 But let him that glorieth glory in this, that he understandeth and knoweth me, that I am the Lord which exercise lovingkindness, judgment, and righteousness, in the earth: for in these things I delight, saith the Lord. 25 Behold, the days come, saith the Lord, that I will punish all them which are circumcised with the uncircumcised; 26 Egypt, and Judah, and Edom, and the children of Ammon, and Moab, and all that are in the utmost corners, that dwell in the wilderness: for all these nations are uncircumcised, and all the house of Israel are uncircumcised in the heart.

9.17-26 Mourning women. In the Eastern culture professional mourners are common. The more wealthy the patron, the larger contingent of mourners. Here Jeremiah is saying the death will be so widespread, it will require the whole female population to lament the dead. The dead will be so many they will not be able to get them all buried, and they will lay unburied in the countryside. In that day the most valuable thing will not be wisdom, fame, or money. The most valuable thing will be to know the Lord. Egypt, Judah, and Edom are being gathered to punish Judah. The most valuable things in the eyes of God are loving-kindness, judgment, and righteousness. Judah has failed to embrace these and now is to suffer the consequences.

Chapter 10

10.1-16 Hear ye the word which the Lord speaketh unto you, O house of Israel: 2 Thus saith the Lord, Learn not the way of the heathen, and be not dismayed at the signs of heaven; for the heathen are dismayed at them. 3 For the customs of the people are vain: for one cutteth a tree out of the forest, the work of the hands of the workman, with the axe. 4 They deck it with silver and with gold; they fasten it with nails and with hammers, that it move not. 5 They are upright as the palm tree, but speak not: they must needs be borne, because they cannot go. Be not afraid of them; for they cannot do evil, neither also is it in them to do good. 6 Forasmuch as there is none like unto thee, O Lord; thou art great, and thy name is great in might. 7 Who would not fear thee, O King of nations? for to thee doth it appertain: forasmuch as among all the wise men of the nations, and in all their kingdoms, there is none like unto thee. 8 But they are altogether brutish and foolish: the stock is a doctrine of vanities. 9 Silver spread into plates is brought from Tarshish, and gold from Uphaz, the work of the workman, and of the hands of the founder: blue and purple is their clothing: they are all the work of cunning men. 10 But the Lord is the true God, he is the living God, and an everlasting king: at his wrath the earth shall tremble, and the nations shall not be able to abide his indignation. 11 Thus shall ye say unto them, The gods that have not made the heavens and the earth, even they shall perish from the earth, and from under these heavens. 12 He hath made the earth by his power, he hath established the world by his wisdom, and hath stretched out the heavens by his discretion. 13 When he uttereth his voice, there is a multitude of waters in the heavens, and he causeth the vapours to ascend from the ends of the earth; he maketh lightnings with rain, and bringeth forth the wind out of his treasures. 14 Every man is brutish in his knowledge: every founder is confounded by the graven image: for his molten image is falsehood, and there is no breath in them. 15 They are vanity, and the work of errors: in the time of their visitation they shall perish. 16 The portion of Jacob is not like them: for he is the former of all things; and Israel is the rod of his inheritance: The Lord of hosts is his name.

10.1-16 The sign of heaven. God admonishes his people to not learn the way of the heathen. The heathen nations were dismayed at the signs of the heavens because of unbelief and rebellion against God. God uses the natural world and natural elements at times to show his power to build faith and confidence. This is seen many times in scripture. One example is Elijah on Mt Carmel. The heathen would take an evergreen tree and cut it out of the forest, place it in their home, decorate it with gold and silver, and then worship it. These practices become popular with the people of God and Jeremiah was condemning it. The silver and the gold used to adorn these trees was the work of man's hands (9). When compared to the power of God who made the earth and heavens, these false gods are seen for what they are: graven images. Israel is told to stay true to God and avoid these graven images, which are man made.

10.17-25 Gather up thy wares out of the land, O inhabitant of the fortress. 18 For thus saith the Lord, Behold, I will sling out the inhabitants of the land at this once, and will distress them, that they may find it so. 19 Woe is me for my hurt! my wound is grievous; but I said, Truly this is a grief, and I must bear it. 20 My tabernacle is spoiled, and all my cords are broken: my children are gone forth of me, and they are not: there is none to stretch forth my tent any more, and to set up my curtains. 21 For the pastors are become brutish, and have not sought the Lord: therefore they shall not prosper, and all their flocks shall be scattered. 22 Behold, the noise of the bruit is come, and a great commotion out of the north country, to make the cities of Judah desolate, and a den of dragons. 23 O Lord, I know that the way of man is not in himself: it is not in man that walketh to direct his steps. 24 O Lord, correct me, but with judgment; not in thine anger, lest thou bring me to nothing. 25 Pour out thy fury upon the heathen that know thee not, and upon the families that call not on thy name: for they have eaten up Jacob, and devoured him, and consumed him, and have made his habitation desolate.

10.17-25 Pastors. The cause of the apostasy surrounding Jeremiah was the product of brutish pastors. These pastors (shepherd) were brutish (feeding themselves). Jeremiah seeks God's mercy when God pours out His judgment. The influence of leaders can never be underestimated. This principal is an ongoing theme in the Bible. From the days of the Judges, through the prophets, and into the New Testament, the leaders took the populace down. Jesus reserved His harshest condemnation for these types of leaders (Mt 23.1-36). Eight times Jesus pronounces woe upon these false leaders. As the pastors of Jeremiah's day, and as the religious leaders of Jesus' day, led many astray, this holds true today as well. Matthew records, many will say in that day Lord, Lord, have we not prophesied in thy name? Jesus' answer is depart from me, I never knew you (Mt 7.21-23). Paul told Timothy he would not only save them that heard him, but would also save himself (1 Tim 4.16). The goal of every pastor must be to speak the oracles of God faithfully, in doing this he will save those that hear him and also save himself.

Chapter 11

11.1-10 The word that came to Jeremiah from the Lord saying, 2 Hear ye the words of this covenant, and speak unto the men of Judah, and to the inhabitants of Jerusalem; 3 And say thou unto them, Thus saith the Lord God of Israel; Cursed be the man that obeyeth not the words of this covenant, 4 Which I commanded your fathers in the day that I brought them forth out of the land of Egypt, from the iron furnace, saying, Obey my voice, and do them, according to all which I command you: so shall ye be my people, and I will be your God: 5 That I may perform the oath which I have sworn unto your fathers, to give them a land flowing with milk and honey, as it is this day. Then answered I, and said, So be it, O Lord. 6 Then the Lord said unto me, Proclaim all these words in the cities of Judah, and in the streets of Jerusalem, saying, Hear ye the words of this covenant, and do them. 7 For I earnestly protested unto your fathers in the day that I brought them up out of the land of Egypt, even unto this day, rising early and protesting, saying, Obey my voice. 8 Yet they obeyed not, nor inclined their ear, but walked every one in the imagination of their evil heart: therefore I will bring upon them all the words of this covenant, which I commanded them to do: but they did them not. 9 And the Lord said unto me, A conspiracy is found among the men of Judah, and among the inhabitants of Jerusalem. 10 They are turned back to the iniquities of their forefathers, which refused to hear my words; and they went after other gods to serve them: the house of Israel and the house of Judah have broken my covenant which I made with their fathers.

11.1-10 The covenant. In this chapter God charges Judah with not keeping the covenant He instituted, and their forefathers agreed on. God reveals their false loyalties. God says cursed is the man that kept not the covenant. This people had not made the covenant, but God considered it binding because their fathers agreed to it. God was still expecting them to honor a covenant made almost a thousand years before. Here it is called a conspiracy (treason) against God Himself.

11.11-17 Therefore thus saith the Lord, Behold, I will bring evil upon them, which they shall not be able to escape; and though they shall cry unto me, I will not hearken unto them. 12 Then shall the cities of Judah and inhabitants of Jerusalem go, and cry unto the gods unto whom they offer incense: but they shall not save them at all in the time of their trouble. 13 For according to the number of thy cities were thy gods, O Judah; and according to the number of the streets of Jerusalem have ye set up altars to that shameful thing, even altars to burn incense unto Baal. 14 Therefore pray not thou for this people, neither lift up a cry or prayer for them: for I will not hear them in the time that they cry unto me for their trouble. 15 What hath my beloved to do in mine house, seeing she hath wrought lewdness with many, and the holy flesh is passed from thee? when thou doest evil, then thou rejoicest. 16 The Lord called thy name, A green olive tree, fair, and of goodly fruit: with the noise of a great tumult he hath kindled fire upon it, and the branches of it are broken. 17 For the Lord of hosts, that planted thee, hath pronounced evil against thee, for the evil of the house of Israel and of the house of Judah, which they have done against themselves to provoke me to anger in offering incense unto Baal.

11.11-17 Dt. 27.26 had declared, cursed be he that confirmeth not all the words of this law and do them. This was Judah's sin. The covenant was an agreement between almighty God and mortal man. God had kept his part of the agreement and had clearly warned if man did not keep his part then calamity would ensue. That day had arrived. God orders Jeremiah to not pray for these people for God is set in His mind to send judgment. God has decided He will not hear them when they cry. Some may say it is never too late to pray, but this interchange proves there are times when prayer will no longer help. This exchange seems to be in the early days of Jeremiah's ministry while he is still in Anathoth, his hometown. This would mean it would be during the time when Josiah was renewing the covenant with the nation, so Jeremiah is supporting the reforms put in by the young King Josiah.

11.18-23 And the Lord hath given me knowledge of it, and I know it: then thou shewedst me their doings. 19 But I was like a lamb or an ox that is brought to the slaughter; and I knew not that they had devised devices against me, saying, Let us destroy the tree with the fruit thereof, and let us cut him off from the land of the living, that his name may be no more remembered. 20 But, O Lord of hosts, that judgest righteously, that triest the reins and the heart, let me see thy vengeance on them: for unto thee have I revealed my cause. 21 Therefore thus saith the Lord of the men of Anathoth, that seek thy life,

saying, Prophesy not in the name of the Lord, that thou die not by our hand: 22 Therefore thus saith the Lord of hosts, Behold, I will punish them: the young men shall die by the sword; their sons and their daughters shall die by famine: 23 And there shall be no remnant of them: for I will bring evil upon the men of Anathoth, even the year of their visitation.

11.18-23 The men of Anathoth. The men of Jeremiah's hometown determine they do not want to hear these prophecies. It is probable they were also priests. Their answer is to kill Jeremiah and shut him up. Jeremiah sees himself as a lamb to the slaughter. God had likened them to an olive tree, so they now say they will cut off this tree and it's fruit. God reveals their machinations to Jeremiah. God protects His prophet and turns the wicked plans back on these evil men. Once again we see in Jeremiah a glimpse of Jesus. Jesus' brothers also turned against Him and one time in Nazareth even tried to kill Him. Jesus simply disappeared out of their midst. Jeremiah imprecates vengeance upon the men of Anathoth, and in a spirit of prophecy, foretells their utter ruin and destruction. Their ruin and annihilation insures there will be no remnant of these wicked men. Their seminal line is cut off forever. This was fulfilled when the invasion of Babylon occurred in the days of Zedekiah. This severe action by God displays how God feels when people do not want to hear the word from God. It also reveals how God reacts when people take it upon themselves to withstand a God called man.

Chapter 12

12.1-4 Righteous art thou, O Lord, when I plead with thee: yet let me talk with thee of thy judgments: Wherefore doth the way of the wicked prosper? wherefore are all they happy that deal very treacherously? 2 Thou hast planted them, yea, they have taken root: they grow, yea, they bring forth fruit: thou art near in their mouth, and far from their reins. 3 But thou, O Lord, knowest me: thou hast seen me, and tried mine heart toward thee: pull them out like sheep for the slaughter, and prepare them for the day of slaughter. 4 How long shall the land mourn, and the herbs of every field wither, for the wickedness of them that dwell therein? the beasts are consumed, and the birds; because they said, He shall not see our last end.

12.1-4 Jeremiah complains. This is still in the same context about the men of Anathoth. In chapter 11 Jeremiah is not happy because these false prophets of his hometown are blessed. He appeals to God because he has done righteously and they are wicked men. He wants God to slaughter them. Jeremiah asks the age-old question of every time period, why do the wicked prosper? God has certain laws he instituted in this universe. For example; the law of gravity or the law of thermal dynamics. These laws are consistent and universal. Sometimes wicked men follow laws of financial blessing. It is not that God is blessing them as much as they have discovered how to be blessed and get riches. God will judge the wicked in His own time. The wicked will pay for their wickedness, but God does not mete out judgment according to our wishes. In this, like all matters, God is sovereign.

12.5-6 If thou hast run with the footmen, and they have wearied thee, then how canst thou contend with horses? and if in the land of peace, wherein thou trustedst, they wearied thee, then how wilt thou do in the swelling of Jordan? 6 For even thy brethren, and the house of thy father, even they have dealt treacherously with thee; yea, they have called a multitude after thee: believe them not, though they speak fair words unto thee.

12.5-6 God answers. God is telling Jeremiah if this wearies you, you should know it will get worse. Jeremiah had not even left his hometown yet and there was a whole nation to deal with. If he is overwhelmed with these false prophets at the beginning, what will happen when he encounters the swelling of Jordan? This is a metaphor of a multitude of false prophets who will later imprison Jeremiah, and cause him immense distress.

12.7-13 I have forsaken mine house, I have left mine heritage; I have given the dearly beloved of my soul into the hand of her enemies. 8 Mine heritage is unto me as a lion in the forest; it crieth out against me: therefore have I hated it. 9 Mine heritage is unto me as a speckled bird, the birds round about are against her; come ye, assemble all the beasts of the field, come to devour. 10 Many pastors have destroyed my vineyard, they have

trodden my portion under foot, they have made my pleasant portion a desolate wilderness. 11 They have made it desolate, and being desolate it mourneth unto me; the whole land is made desolate, because no man layeth it to heart. 12 The spoilers are come upon all high places through the wilderness: for the sword of the Lord shall devour from the one end of the land even to the other end of the land: no flesh shall have peace. 13 They have sown wheat, but shall reap thorns: they have put themselves to pain, but shall not profit: and they shall be ashamed of your revenues because of the fierce anger of the Lord.

12.7-13 The speckled bird. God declares His heritage is as a speckled bird. The word usage here invites the meaning of a bird of prey. Judah has hunted far afield like a hawk and fed on dead carcasses. Now Judah will become the prey and the other birds of prey are invited to come and devour her. Once again the cause of Judah's idolatry is laid at the feet of the pastors. Leaders both civil and religious have caused her to go astray. Spoilers are on their way and the crops will bring no revenue.

12.14-17 Thus saith the Lord against all mine evil neighbours, that touch the inheritance which I have caused my people Israel to inherit; Behold, I will pluck them out of their land, and pluck out the house of Judah from among them. 15 And it shall come to pass, after that I have plucked them out I will return, and have compassion on them, and will bring them again, every man to his heritage, and every man to his land. 16 And it shall come to pass, if they will diligently learn the ways of my people, to swear by my name, The Lord liveth; as they taught my people to swear by Baal; then shall they be built in the midst of my people. 17 But if they will

not obey, I will utterly pluck up and destroy that nation, saith the Lord.

12.14-17 The flood of judgment. When the judgment comes it will overflow Judah and encompass the surrounding nations as well. The evil neighbors will be caught up in the storm of trouble. The storm will pass as all storms do. After the storm Judah will be returned to her land. The evil nations around will also be given the opportunity to learn the ways of the Lord. These nations taught Judah to swear by Baal, now Judah will teach them to trust in Jehovah, if they will listen. If not, these nations will be annulled. Judah will again gain world supremacy and lead the nations of the world to God.

Chapter 13

13.1-11 Thus saith the Lord unto me, Go and get thee a linen girdle, and put it upon thy loins, and put it not in water. 2 So I got a girdle according to the word of the Lord, and put it on my loins. 3 And the word of the Lord came unto me the second time, saying, 4 Take the girdle that thou hast got, which is upon thy loins, and arise, go to Euphrates, and hide it there in a hole of the rock. 5 So I went, and hid it by Euphrates, as the Lord commanded me. 6 And it came to pass after many days, that the Lord said unto me, Arise, go to Euphrates, and take the girdle from thence, which I commanded thee to hide there. 7 Then I went to Euphrates, and digged, and took the girdle from the place where I had hid it: and, behold, the girdle was marred, it was profitable for nothing. 8 Then the word of the Lord came unto me, saying, 9 Thus saith the Lord, After this manner will I mar the pride of Judah, and the great pride of Jerusalem. 10 This evil people, which refuse to hear my words, which walk in the imagination of their heart, and walk after other gods, to serve them, and to worship them, shall even be as this girdle, which is good for nothing. 11 For as the girdle cleaveth to the loins of a man, so have I caused to cleave unto me the whole house of Israel and the whole house of Judah, saith the Lord; that they might be unto me for a

people, and for a name, and for a praise, and for a glory: but they would not hear.

13.1-11 The girdle. This is a sash worn as a belt or a linen undergarment that stretched from the waist down to mid thigh. Jeremiah was instructed to put this on and go to the Euphrates and hide this girdle in a hole in the rock. He is then told to go and retrieve it. It is now decayed. Jeremiah is here given one of his famous sermons to preach. God says as the girdle cleaveth to the loins of a man, so I have caused the house of Israel and Judah to cleave to me. God is telling Judah that He will bring their pride to nothing and their haughtiness to the ground. Again God calls for repentance. Judah is apostrophized; some of her will be eliminated. She will be but a contraction of her original potential. Yet this message shows the striking imagery of how God has kept His people close to him in intimacy. God desires intimacy with His chosen people.

13.12-14 Therefore thou shalt speak unto them this word; Thus saith the Lord God of Israel, Every bottle shall be filled with wine: and they shall say unto thee, Do we not certainly know that every bottle shall be filled with wine? 13 Then shalt thou say unto them, Thus saith the Lord, Behold, I will fill all the inhabitants of this land, even the kings that sit upon David's throne, and the priests, and the prophets, and all the inhabitants of Jerusalem, with drunkenness. 14 And I will dash them one against another, even the fathers and the sons together, saith the Lord: I will not pity, nor spare, nor have mercy, but destroy them.

13.12-14 Wine. The two symbols of the covenant were the fig tree and the vine. These two symbols represent fruitfulness and blessing. When the elements of the basic covenant were abused for personal aggrandizement God became angry. Judah had become an unfruitful vine. The people had become drunkards. Jeremiah condemns the populace for perverting a covenant symbol into personal satisfaction. Without this simple understanding, the anger of God seems disproportionate.

13.15-21 Hear ye, and give ear; be not proud: for the Lord hath spoken. 16 Give glory to the Lord your God, before he cause darkness, and before your feet stumble upon the dark mountains, and, while ye look for light, he turn it into the shadow of death, and make it gross darkness. 17 But if ye will not hear it, my soul shall weep in secret places for your pride; and mine eye shall weep sore, and run down with tears, because the Lord's flock is carried away captive. 18 Say unto the king and to the queen, Humble yourselves, sit down: for your principalities shall come down, even the crown of your glory. 19 The cities of the south shall be shut up, and none shall open them: Judah shall be carried away captive all of it, it shall be wholly carried away captive. 20 Lift up your eyes, and behold them that come from the north: where is the flock that was given thee, thy beautiful flock? 21 What wilt thou say when he shall punish thee? for thou hast taught them to be captains, and as chief over thee: shall not sorrows take thee, as a woman in travail?

13.15-21 Exile. Pride goeth before destruction. This axiom is here proven true. The pride of Judah has positioned her to fall, and the fall is mighty. Judah will be carried away captive for 70 years and the Jubilee years that were to be celebrated, but apparently were not, will be accomplished. The land will lie fallow. God will not allow his directives to be ignored. The captivity accomplished several things simultaneously. It punished Judah for her backsliding. It also gave the land the 70 years rest the years of Jubilee would have provided had they been observed. Maybe the most important accomplishment of the captivity was the abolishment of idolatry. Upon return from captivity, Israel has never again been tempted to worship idols. This blight on her history marred her for over 1000 years, but the captivity finally cured this in the heart of the Jewish people. The exile to Israel was like chemotherapy to a cancer patient. It cured the cancer of idolatry. To this day Israel is in remission concerning idolatry.

13.22-27 And if thou say in thine heart, Wherefore come these things upon me? For the greatness of thine iniquity are thy skirts discovered, and thy heels made bare. 23 Can the Ethiopian change his skin, or the leopard his spots? then may ye also do good, that are accustomed to do evil. 24 Therefore will I scatter them as the stubble that passeth away by the wind of the wilderness. 25 This is thy lot, the portion of thy measures from me, saith the Lord; because thou hast forgotten me, and trusted in falsehood. 26 Therefore will I discover thy skirts upon thy face, that thy shame may appear. 27 I have seen thine adulteries, and thy neighings, the lewdness of thy whoredom, and thine abominations on the hills in the fields. Woe unto thee, O Jerusalem! wilt thou not be made clean? when shall it once be?

13.22-27 The lingering image of captivity inspires Jeremiah to finish out this portion of his prophecy with analogy. The people have stumbled on the dark mountains. They have groped in the darkness. No light came and they were in the very shadow of death. Jeremiah weeps. In the privacy of his soul Jeremiah sees the long hard road ahead, and it overwhelms him with sore weeping. Fresh on the heels of this emotion is the flitting thought, can an Ethiopian change his skin, or a leopard his spots? This saying has become common vernacular for it's succinct meaning. This people have been held close by God for 1000 years (the girdle), they have mongrelized the hallowed sign of the covenant (the wine), they are now on schedule to be deported to Babylon, can they change? With deep sorrow and futility Jeremiah faces the unwanted answer. With weeping in secret places, the prophet faces the conclusion. Woe unto thee, O Jerusalem. This nation cannot change without the purge of the captivity.

Chapter 14

14.1-6 The word of the Lord that came to Jeremiah concerning the dearth. 2 Judah mourneth, and the gates thereof languish; they are black unto the ground; and the cry of Jerusalem is gone up. 3 And their nobles have sent their little ones to the waters: they came to the pits, and found no water; they returned with their vessels empty; they were ashamed and confounded, and covered their heads. 4 Because the ground is chapt, for there was no rain in the earth, the plowmen were ashamed, they covered their heads. 5 Yea, the hind also calved in the field, and forsook it, because there was no grass. 6 And the wild asses did stand in the high places, they snuffed up the wind like dragons; their eyes did fail, because there was no grass.

14.1-6. Famine. Famine is a common event associated with God withholding his blessings. When God blesses He sends rain and abundance. The crops are plentiful and abundant. Famine is a result of no rain, no crops, and no blessings. The examples of what occurs in the Bible during famine is disturbing. Unnatural acts abound during famine. Even the animal kingdom acted unnatural, the deer left their fawns in the field for lack of food. In some cases, people actually ate their own children. In this setting Jeremiah deals with a drought that produces a famine. He describes the distress of the people. The nobility were affected by the famine as well as the common people. Famine is no respecter of persons. Jeremiah informs that the ground could not be plowed (illustrating the heart of the people). There was no grass and the animals were starving (the spiritual condition of the people). Jeremiah prays for rain for the Lord's namesake in the eyes of the people.

14.7-12 O Lord, though our iniquities testify against us, do thou it for thy name's sake: for our backslidings are many; we have sinned against thee. 8 O the hope of Israel, the saviour thereof in time of trouble, why shouldest thou be as a stranger in the land, and as a wayfaring man that turneth aside to tarry for a night? 9 Why shouldest thou be as a man astonied, as a mighty man that cannot save? yet thou, O Lord, art in the midst of us, and we are called by thy name; leave us not. 10 Thus saith the Lord unto this people, Thus have they loved to wander, they have not refrained their feet, therefore the Lord doth not accept them; he will now remember their iniquity, and visit their sins. 11 Then said the Lord unto me, Pray not for this people for their good. 12 When they fast, I will not hear their cry; and when they offer burnt offering and an oblation, I will not accept them: but I will consume them by the sword, and by the famine, and by the pestilence.

14.7-12 The lament. Jeremiah is well known for his lamentations. Many of his laments are gathered together and placed in the book of Lamentations. To lament is to express deep grief. It is to attempt to express what cannot be said. It is the art of putting unspeakable feelings that are cascading through your emotions into some form of expression. It is more than just writing as in a diary or journal. Jeremiah had been told to not intercede for this people, but he is overcome with unspeakable emotional pain and pens this lament. God rejects his request and reminds him it is useless to pray for this obdurate people. It is interesting that God will not hear the lament of Jeremiah due to His anger; God himself then gives Jeremiah a lament in verse 17.

14.13-16 Then said I, Ah, Lord God! behold, the prophets say unto them, Ye shall not see the sword, neither shall ye have famine; but I will give you assured peace in this place. 14 Then the Lord said unto me, The prophets prophesy lies in my name: I sent them not, neither have I commanded them, neither spake unto them: they prophesy unto you a false vision and divination, and a thing of nought, and the deceit of their heart. 15 Therefore thus saith the Lord concerning the prophets that prophesy in my name, and I sent them not, yet they say, Sword and famine shall not be in this land; By sword and famine shall those prophets be consumed. 16 And the people to whom they prophesy shall be cast out in the streets of Jerusalem because of the famine and the sword; and they shall have none to bury them, them, their wives, nor their sons, nor their daughters: for I will pour their wickedness upon them.

14.13-16 False prophets. Few people in the Bible incite God's wrath like false prophets. There are multiple reasons for this. One reason being they give the people a false hope. They speak spiritual mirages that lure God's people into the dry places. These false preachers speak in God's name thus making God a liar in the eyes of the people. They say peace and prosperity to the people, when the people's future is actually judgment and famine. On many occasions God uses their own words to indict them and judge them. Here God does this. The prophecy these liars give is turned back upon them to become their own retributive justice. Their own mouth and lying heart become their nemesis.

14.17-22 Therefore thou shalt say this word unto them; Let mine eyes run down with tears night and day, and let them not cease: for the virgin daughter of my people is broken with a great breach, with a very grievous blow. 18 If I go forth into the field, then behold the slain with the sword! and if I enter into the city, then behold them that are sick with famine! yea, both the prophet and the priest go about into a land that they know not. 19 Hast thou utterly rejected Judah? hath thy soul lothed Zion? why hast thou smitten us, and there is no healing for us? we looked for peace, and there is no good; and for the time of healing, and behold trouble! 20 We acknowledge, O Lord, our wickedness, and the iniquity of our fathers: for we have sinned against thee. 21 Do not abhor us, for thy name's sake, do not disgrace the throne of thy glory: remember, break not thy covenant with us. 22 Are there any among the vanities of the Gentiles that can cause rain? or can the heavens give showers? art not thou he, O Lord our God? therefore we will wait upon thee: for thou hast made all these things.

14.17-22 God's lament. God in his mercy sees the heartbreak of His faithful prophet. So God directs the lament rather than tell the prophet to be quiet. It is as though God sees Jeremiah's need to get this emotion out so God redirects it to a proper channel. The lament shifts from a pleading for the people, to a grieving for the people. Jeremiah prophesied during the reign of the Good King Josiah. We are not privy to know when this passage was penned for the works of Jeremiah are not consecutive in how they are placed in the book. Was this before the reforms of Josiah? Was this after

Josiah had fallen in battle on the plains of Megiddo? In the final lament that God speaks, He challenges the people to find a god among those vanities that can send rain and remove the famine. God challenges Judah to see if these false gods have any warrant ability.

Chapter 15

15.1-9 Then said the Lord unto me, Though Moses and Samuel stood before me, yet my mind could not be toward this people: cast them out of my sight, and let them go forth. 2 And it shall come to pass, if they say unto thee, Whither shall we go forth? then thou shalt tell them, Thus saith the Lord; Such as are for death, to death; and such as are for the sword, to the sword; and such as are for the famine, to the famine; and such as are for the captivity, to the captivity. 3 And I will appoint over them four kinds, saith the Lord: the sword to slay, and the dogs to tear, and the fowls of the heaven, and the beasts of the earth, to devour and destroy. 4 And I will cause them to be removed into all kingdoms of the earth, because of Manasseh the son of Hezekiah king of Judah, for that which he did in Jerusalem. 5 For who shall have pity upon thee, O Jerusalem? or who shall bemoan thee? or who shall go aside to ask how thou doest? 6 Thou hast forsaken me, saith the Lord, thou art gone backward: therefore will I stretch out my hand against thee, and destroy thee; I am weary with repenting. 7 And I will fan them with a fan in the gates of the land; I will bereave them of children, I will destroy my people since they return not from their ways. 8 Their widows are increased to me above the sand of the seas: I have brought upon

them against the mother of the young men a spoiler at noonday: I have caused him to fall upon it suddenly, and terrors upon the city. 9 She that hath borne seven languisheth: she hath given up the ghost; her sun is gone down while it was yet day: she hath been ashamed and confounded: and the residue of them will I deliver to the sword before their enemies, saith the Lord.

15.1-9 Repenting. God is weary. God is frustrated. God declares the most righteous people imaginable would not deter his decision. His mind is made up. One of the big causes, if not the most prominent cause, is the reign of Manasseh. God declares the prayers of the two men who changed God's mind, Moses and Samuel, would not affect Him. God has appointed four mediums of destruction. First the sword, second the dogs to tear and eat the corpses, third the birds and beasts of prey like jackals, and lastly others that will finish the job. God is unequivocally telling the nation the issue is settled. There is no more option of delay. We are still reading some of Jeremiah's lament, which includes short dirges, oracles of judgment, and confessions. The "hope being lost" issue is illustrated by a mother of seven who no longer even tries. Her light is gone out and hope is gone. She has lost the spirit most women have: example of Rizpah in 2 S 21.8-11.

15.10-14 Woe is me, my mother, that thou hast borne me a man of strife and a man of contention to the whole earth! I have neither lent on usury, nor men have lent to me on usury; yet every one of them doth curse me. 11 The Lord said, Verily it shall be well with thy remnant; verily I will cause the enemy to entreat thee well in the time of evil and in the time of affliction. 12 Shall iron break the northern iron and the steel? 13 Thy substance and thy treasures will I give to the spoil without price,

and that for all thy sins, even in all thy borders. 14 And I will make thee to pass with thine enemies into a land which thou knowest not: for a fire is kindled in mine anger, which shall burn upon you.

15.10-14 Jeremiah complains. This tragic scene of wholesale loss and destruction is too much for Jeremiah. Jeremiah attacks his mother for bearing him. His distress is overflowing in an emotional outburst. It seems Jeremiah is at the lowest point of his life. He defends himself. He is not a bad person that deserves what is happening to him. He feels friendless, discouraged, frustrated and despairs of life. God has not forsaken him. God lets Jeremiah know that Jeremiah will also accompany them into captivity. The role of a true shepherd is to be with his flock even in the most perilous of times. Jeremiah trudges on as a faithful servant.

15.15-18 O Lord, thou knowest: remember me, and visit me, and revenge me of my persecutors; take me not away in thy longsuffering: know that for thy sake I have suffered rebuke. 16 Thy words were found, and I did eat them; and thy word was unto me the joy and rejoicing of mine heart: for I am called by thy name, O Lord God of hosts. 17 I sat not in the assembly of the mockers, nor rejoiced; I sat alone because of thy hand: for thou hast filled me with indignation. 18 Why is my pain perpetual, and my wound incurable, which refuseth to be healed? wilt thou be altogether unto me as a liar, and as waters that fail?

15.15-18 Despair reaches the bottom. It these few verses we see the relationship Jeremiah has with God. Jeremiah lashes out. He even goes so far as to accuse God of being a liar. The original vision of building the old places seems so impossible at the moment. He is angry at God for not revenging him against his tormentors. Jeremiah has survived by eating the word. The lesson, among others here, is that the word can and will sustain us in the darkest of times. When you want to quit or die, it is the word that sustains. The Bible is replete with others who mirror this principal. An example would be David at the cave of Adullam, and when Absalom rebelled and tried to take the kingdom.

15.19-21 Therefore thus saith the Lord, If thou return, then will I bring thee again, and thou shalt stand before me: and if thou take forth the precious from the vile, thou shalt be as my mouth: let them return unto thee; but return not thou unto them. 20 And I will make thee unto this people a fenced brasen wall: and they shall fight against thee, but they shall not prevail against thee: for I am with thee to save thee and to deliver thee, saith the Lord. 21 And I will deliver thee out of the hand of the wicked, and I will redeem thee out of the hand of the terrible.

15.19-21 Jeremiah the servant. God is reminding Jeremiah this is not about Jeremiah. God is saying do what I tell you. Say what I tell you to say. I will sustain you, and make you a brazen wall. These naysayers will not succeed against you. The road to deliverance is through obedience and submission to the will of God. God will preserve and protect his prophet. Then God will vindicate his boy prophet. Jeremiah is told to not go back and speak to them again.

Chapter 16

16.1-9 The word of the Lord came also unto me, saying, 2 Thou shalt not take thee a wife, neither shalt thou have sons or daughters in this place. 3 For thus saith the Lord concerning the sons and concerning the daughters that are born in this place, and concerning their mothers that bare them, and concerning their fathers that begat them in this land; 4 They shall die of grievous deaths; they shall not be lamented; neither shall they be buried; but they shall be as dung upon the face of the earth: and they shall be consumed by the sword, and by famine; and their carcases shall be meat for the fowls of heaven, and for the beasts of the earth. 5 For thus saith the Lord, Enter not into the house of mourning, neither go to lament nor bemoan them: for I have taken away my peace from this people, saith the Lord, even lovingkindness and mercies. 6 Both the great and the small shall die in this land: they shall not be buried, neither shall men lament for them, nor cut themselves, nor make themselves bald for them: 7 Neither shall men tear themselves for them in mourning, to comfort them for the dead; neither shall men give them the cup of consolation to drink for their father or for their mother. 8 Thou shalt not also go into the house of feasting, to sit with them to eat and to drink. 9 For thus saith the Lord of hosts, the God of

Israel; Behold, I will cause to cease out of this place in your eyes, and in your days, the voice of mirth, and the voice of gladness, the voice of the bridegroom, and the voice of the bride.

16.1-9 Jeremiah's personal life. Jeremiah is forbidden to get married or attend social events either happy or sad. The deaths that are coming are going to be so heinous that God forbids the prophet to contribute to them. He could not go to the house of sadness because it would not compare to the coming sadness. He was told to not go to the house of feasting because the nation was going to face hard and difficult days. The cause of all this was the forsaking of the Lord by the people. The people were forbidden to cut themselves (Lev 19.28) or shave the baldness of the forehead (Deut 14.1). These practices had been forbidden for centuries but apparently the people were still practicing them. These were heathen practices showing passionate mourning for the dead.

16.10-13 And it shall come to pass, when thou shalt shew this people all these words, and they shall say unto thee, Wherefore hath the Lord pronounced all this great evil against us? or what is our iniquity? or what is our sin that we have committed against the Lord our God? 11 Then shalt thou say unto them, Because your fathers have forsaken me, saith the Lord, and have walked after other gods, and have served them, and have worshipped them, and have forsaken me, and have not kept my law; 12 And ye have done worse than your fathers; for, behold, ye walk every one after the imagination of his evil heart, that they may not hearken unto me: 13 Therefore will I cast you out of this land into a land that ye know not, neither ye nor your fathers; and there shall ye serve other gods day and night; where I will not shew you favour.

16.10-13 They asked God why? Jeremiah was instructed that when he was asked why this was happening, to declare plainly it is because you have forsaken the Lord. You have done worse than your fathers. Throughout the history of mankind despite education and progress, man has continued to sin more egregiously.

16.14-15 Therefore, behold, the days come, saith the Lord, that it shall no more be said, The Lord liveth, that brought up the children of Israel out of the land of Egypt; 15 But, The Lord liveth, that brought up the children of Israel from the land of the north, and from all the lands whither he had driven them: and I will bring them again into their land that I gave unto their fathers.

16.14-15 The new mantra. No longer will God be known as the God who brought them out of Egypt, but he will be known as the God who brought them out of the North.

16.16-21 Behold, I will send for many fishers, saith the Lord, and they shall fish them; and after will I send for many hunters, and they shall hunt them from every mountain, and from every hill, and out of the holes of the rocks. 17 For mine eyes are upon all their ways: they are not hid from my face, neither is their iniquity hid from mine eyes. 18 And first I will recompense their iniquity and their sin double; because they have defiled my land, they have filled mine inheritance with the carcases of their detestable and abominable things. 19 O Lord, my strength, and my fortress, and my refuge in the day of affliction, the Gentiles shall come unto thee from the ends of the earth, and shall say, Surely our fathers have inherited lies, vanity, and things wherein there is no profit. 20 Shall a man make gods unto himself, and they are no gods? 21 Therefore, behold, I will this once

cause them to know, I will cause them to know mine hand and my might; and they shall know that my name is The Lord.

16.16-21 Fishers and hunters. God will provide fishers and hunters to seek out his wayward people and punish them. Then the day will come when the anger of God will have burned out and God will bring his people back. God will use this opportunity to reveal himself to the Gentile nations.

Chapter 17

17.1-4 The sin of Judah is written with a pen of iron, and with the point of a diamond: it is graven upon the table of their heart, and upon the horns of your altars; 2 Whilst their children remember their altars and their groves by the green trees upon the high hills. 3 O my mountain in the field, I will give thy substance and all thy treasures to the spoil, and thy high places for sin, throughout all thy borders. 4 And thou, even thyself, shalt discontinue from thine heritage that I gave thee; and I will cause thee to serve thine enemies in the land which thou knowest not: for ye have kindled a fire in mine anger, which shall burn for ever.

17.1-4 The idolatry of Judah. The sin of Judah is ineffaceably graven on their hearts and on their altars. This is the reason Judah must be cast forth among the nations and purged. What is written on the heart is of paramount importance to God. Prov 3.3 and 7.3 speak of what is written on the heart. Judah's sin had become so deeply engraved it could not be removed. Excavations in Judah have uncovered horned altars and on some of these altars there are still blood stains after 2500 years. God left evidence to support his judgment. This heart engraving would ultimately become the message of Jeremiah, and become the basis of the New Covenant.

17.5-8 Thus saith the Lord; Cursed be the man that trusteth in man, and maketh flesh his arm, and whose heart departeth from the Lord. 6 For he shall be like the heath in the desert, and shall not see when good cometh; but shall inhabit the parched places in the wilderness, in a salt land and not inhabited. 7 Blessed is the man that trusteth in the Lord, and whose hope the Lord is. 8 For he shall be as a tree planted by the waters, and that spreadeth out her roots by the river, and shall not see when heat cometh, but her leaf shall be green; and shall not be careful in the year of drought, neither shall cease from yielding fruit.

17.5-8 Trees planted by the water. This analogy is a familiar one in the plan of God. It speaks of longevity, durability, and fruitfulness. Judah was trusting in human treaties with the nations around, so she was not guaranteed to stand through the storms. He shall be like the heath, which is a solitary tree in the desert. The contrast is to a lone tree that struggles to survive (human help), verses a tree that flourishes and never fails (God's help).

17.9-10 The heart is deceitful above all things, and desperately wicked: who can know it? 10 I the Lord search the heart, I try the reins, even to give every man according to his ways, and according to the fruit of his doings.

17.9-10 The heart. This is the subject of this prophecy. This is a flash point not only for this book of prophecy, but for every life of all generations. From the opening verses about what is written on the heart, to the fact no one ever truly knows their heart, this subject is the focal point of the future. The Word of God written on stone had not produced trees that endured and bare fruit through every drought and famine. When the Word of God is written on the heart instead of stone, faithful trees will be planted that will endure every season and remain fruitful. No subject is of greater interest to God than the condition of the heart. The word used here, deceitful, has the connotation of swelling which indicates tripping a person up. This is a nod to Jacob their forebear, who was a supplanter at heart. The connection is Judah's heart was as Jacob's heart. Judah was following Jacob's deceit, not Israel's faith.

17.11-14 As the partridge sitteth on eggs, and hatcheth them not; so he that getteth riches, and not by right, shall leave them in the midst of his days, and at his end shall be a fool. 12 A glorious high throne from the beginning is the place of our sanctuary. 13 O Lord, the hope of Israel, all that forsake thee shall be ashamed, and they that depart from me shall be written in the earth, because they have forsaken the Lord, the fountain of living waters. 14 Heal me, O Lord, and I shall be healed; save me, and I shall be saved: for thou art my praise.

17.11-14 Misplaced hope. At first glance this verse seems arbitrary and random. The subject here is the heart. Judah had a misplaced hope in her affections and her trust. This will produce nothing as the Partridge who does not hatch her eggs. The musings of Judah's heart is being revealed and their misplaced hopes will not produce the desired ends.

17.15-18 Behold, they say unto me, Where is the word of the Lord? let it come now. 16 As for me, I have not hastened from being a pastor to follow thee: neither

have I desired the woeful day; thou knowest: that which came out of my lips was right before thee. 17 Be not a terror unto me: thou art my hope in the day of evil. 18 Let them be confounded that persecute me, but let not me be confounded: let them be dismayed, but let not me be dismayed: bring upon them the day of evil, and destroy them with double destruction.

17.15-18 Preservation. Jeremiah accepts he will not escape the coming judgment so he prays for preservation. He seeks divine favor in the midst of divine judgment. He presents his appeal of being a faithful pastor. He is seeking the secret place of the most high, a shelter from the storm. He does not ask to be delivered from the storm but rather to be safely brought through the coming holocaust. Jeremiah had stated in verse 7 that blessed is the man that trusts in the Lord. His appeal to God is to prove that by blessing him in the midst of the gathering storm clouds of captivity.

17.19-27 Thus said the Lord unto me; Go and stand in the gate of the children of the people, whereby the kings of Judah come in, and by the which they go out, and in all the gates of Jerusalem; 20 And say unto them, Hear ye the word of the Lord, ye kings of Judah, and all Judah, and all the inhabitants of Jerusalem, that enter in by these gates: 21 Thus saith the Lord; Take heed to yourselves, and bear no burden on the sabbath day, nor bring it in by the gates of Jerusalem; 22 Neither carry forth a burden out of your houses on the sabbath day, neither do ye any work, but hallow ye the sabbath day, as I commanded your fathers. 23 But they obeyed not, neither inclined their ear, but made their neck stiff, that they might not hear, nor receive instruction. 24 And it shall come to pass, if ye diligently hearken unto me,

saith the Lord, to bring in no burden through the gates of this city on the sabbath day, but hallow the sabbath day, to do no work therein; 25 Then shall there enter into the gates of this city kings and princes sitting upon the throne of David, riding in chariots and on horses, they, and their princes, the men of Judah, and the inhabitants of Jerusalem: and this city shall remain for ever. 26 And they shall come from the cities of Judah, and from the places about Jerusalem, and from the land of Benjamin, and from the plain, and from the mountains, and from the south, bringing burnt offerings, and sacrifices, and meat offerings, and incense, and bringing sacrifices of praise, unto the house of the Lord. 27 But if ye will not hearken unto me to hallow the sabbath day, and not to bear a burden, even entering in at the gates of Jerusalem on the sabbath day; then will I kindle a fire in the gates thereof, and it shall devour the palaces of Jerusalem, and it shall not be quenched.

17.19-27 The Sabbath. The recognition of the Sabbath acknowledged God as the creator and preserver of all things. This is the basis of it being required to be hallowed. In this, as in other areas Judah had failed. God will have people that acknowledge Him and His rightful position. Judah is invited to fill that position, but if she defers, God will raise up a people who will fulfill this important covenant role.

Chapter 18

18.1-10 The word which came to Jeremiah from the Lord, saying, 2 Arise, and go down to the potter's house, and there I will cause thee to hear my words. 3 Then I went down to the potter's house, and, behold, he wrought a work on the wheels. 4 And the vessel that he made of clay was marred in the hand of the potter: so he made it again another vessel, as seemed good to the potter to make it. 5 Then the word of the Lord came to me, saying, 6 O house of Israel, cannot I do with you as this potter? saith the Lord. Behold, as the clay is in the potter's hand, so are ye in mine hand, O house of Israel. 7 At what instant I shall speak concerning a nation, and concerning a kingdom, to pluck up, and to pull down, and to destroy it; 8 If that nation, against whom I have pronounced, turn from their evil, I will repent of the evil that I thought to do unto them. 9 And at what instant I shall speak concerning a nation, and concerning a kingdom, to build and to plant it; 10 If it do evil in my sight, that it obey not my voice, then I will repent of the good, wherewith I said I would benefit them.

18.1-10 The potter's house. This is Jeremiah's most famous and well-known sermon. Jeremiah is instructed by the Lord to go to the potter's house and watch the potter work.

The Lord will speak to him there. Upon arriving, Jeremiah sees the vessel being made and there is a problem. The clay is not responding. There is a problem with the texture and quality of the clay. The potter has no option but to crush the incomplete vessel and begin again. This is the succinct message God is repeatedly telling Judah. God has worked with Judah and Judah has not responded so God has no choice except to crush Judah back into a new vessel. This will occur in the coming captivity. God will make a new nation, one without idolatry.

18.11-17 Now therefore go to, speak to the men of Judah, and to the inhabitants of Jerusalem, saying, Thus saith the Lord; Behold, I frame evil against you, and devise a device against you: return ye now every one from his evil way, and make your ways and your doings good. 12 And they said, There is no hope: but we will walk after our own devices, and we will every one do the imagination of his evil heart. 13 Therefore thus saith the Lord; Ask ye now among the heathen, who hath heard such things: the virgin of Israel hath done a very horrible thing. 14 Will a man leave the snow of Lebanon which cometh from the rock of the field? or shall the cold flowing waters that come from another place be forsaken? 15 Because my people hath forgotten me, they have burned incense to vanity, and they have caused them to stumble in their ways from the ancient paths, to walk in paths, in a way not cast up; 16 To make their land desolate, and a perpetual hissing; every one that passeth thereby shall be astonished, and wag his head. 17 I will scatter them as with an east wind before the enemy; I will shew them the back, and not the face, in the day of their calamity.

18.11-17 Obduracy. It is their obdurate attitude that is the flaw in the clay that the potter is rejecting. The Lord clearly says he will forgive if they repent, but their obstinate, bullheaded attitude says no, we will walk after our own heart. This is identified by God to be unusual in all the earth. The nation that was called to be so high, has reached the deepest depth of failure. The divine potter takes His hand and crushes the lump into a heap. In 70 years the divine potter will begin a new vessel.

18.18-23 Then said they, Come and let us devise devices against Jeremiah; for the law shall not perish from the priest, nor counsel from the wise, nor the word from the prophet. Come, and let us smite him with the tongue, and let us not give heed to any of his words. 19 Give heed to me, O Lord, and hearken to the voice of them that contend with me. 20 Shall evil be recompensed for good? for they have digged a pit for my soul. Remember that I stood before thee to speak good for them, and to turn away thy wrath from them. 21 Therefore deliver up their children to the famine, and pour out their blood by the force of the sword; and let their wives be bereaved of their children, and be widows; and let their men be put to death; let their young men be slain by the sword in battle. 22 Let a cry be heard from their houses, when thou shalt bring a troop suddenly upon them: for they have digged a pit to take me, and hid snares for my feet. 23 Yet, Lord, thou knowest all their counsel against me to slay me: forgive not their iniquity, neither blot out their sin from thy sight, but let them be overthrown before thee; deal thus with them in the time of thine anger.

18.18-23 Jeremiah and God agree. On the issue of the people being cast to judgment, Jeremiah now takes the side of God for he has also felt the sting of their betrayal. God has allowed his prophet to feel a smidgen of what God himself has felt, and the minuscule part Jeremiah feels immediately causes him to join God in advocating destruction. The pleading, interceding, weeping Jeremiah now gives way to the indignant, wounded, slighted, misaligned Jeremiah. The prophet who is not allowed to be tainted with human emotion, feels the full blast of what God is feeling. Jeremiah's judgment is swift and conclusive; deliver them to the famine, the sword, and the battle. Jeremiah's mercy, like God's mercy, has run out.

Chapter 19

19.1-2 Thus saith the Lord, Go and get a potter's earthen bottle, and take of the ancients of the people, and of the ancients of the priests; 2 And go forth unto the valley of the son of Hinnom, which is by the entry of the east gate, and proclaim there the words that I shall tell thee,

19.1-2 The bottle. God instructs the prophet to get a bottle from the potter he has just visited in chapter 18 and gather the people for a demonstrated sermon. In the middle of the sermon he is instructed to lift the bottle and break the bottle in their sight. Israel shall be broken by God as the bottle is broken by Jeremiah. This vivid exhibition will imprint on their minds the completeness of their judgment. Judah is broken beyond repair; she cannot be made whole again. As pottery shatters when thrown to the ground, so Judah will be shattered and scattered. The art of the potter could not overcome the flaw of the clay.

19.3-15 And say, Hear ye the word of the Lord, O kings of Judah, and inhabitants of Jerusalem; Thus saith the Lord of hosts, the God of Israel; Behold, I will bring evil upon this place, the which whosoever heareth, his ears shall tingle. 4 Because they have forsaken me, and have estranged this place, and have burned incense in it unto

other gods, whom neither they nor their fathers have known, nor the kings of Judah, and have filled this place with the blood of innocents; 5 They have built also the high places of Baal, to burn their sons with fire for burnt offerings unto Baal, which I commanded not, nor spake it, neither came it into my mind: 6 Therefore, behold, the days come, saith the Lord, that this place shall no more be called Tophet, nor The valley of the son of Hinnom, but The valley of slaughter. 7 And I will make void the counsel of Judah and Jerusalem in this place; and I will cause them to fall by the sword before their enemies, and by the hands of them that seek their lives: and their carcases will I give to be meat for the fowls of the heaven, and for the beasts of the earth. 8 And I will make this city desolate, and an hissing; every one that passeth thereby shall be astonished and hiss because of all the plagues thereof. 9 And I will cause them to eat the flesh of their sons and the flesh of their daughters, and they shall eat every one the flesh of his friend in the siege and straitness, wherewith their enemies, and they that seek their lives, shall straiten them. 10 Then shalt thou break the bottle in the sight of the men that go with thee, 11 And shalt say unto them, Thus saith the Lord of hosts; Even so will I break this people and this city, as one breaketh a potter's vessel, that cannot be made whole again: and they shall bury them in Tophet, till there be no place to bury. 12 Thus will I do unto this place, saith the Lord, and to the inhabitants thereof, and even make this city as Tophet: 13 And the houses of Jerusalem, and the houses of the kings of Judah, shall be defiled as the place of Tophet, because of all the houses upon whose roofs they have burned incense unto all the host of heaven, and have poured out drink offerings unto other gods. 14 Then came Jeremiah from Tophet, whither the Lord had sent him to prophesy; and he stood in the court of the

Lord's house; and said to all the people, 15 Thus saith the Lord of hosts, the God of Israel; Behold, I will bring upon this city and upon all her towns all the evil that I have pronounced against it, because they have hardened their necks, that they might not hear my words.

19.3-15 The ears shall tingle. This axiom reflects news so bad that the ears of people shall tingle. This expression is used to refer to a harsh, ringing judgment announcement. The idea is to vibrate or rattle like when teeth chatter or ears get red with shame. The people have done unspeakable atrocities unto God. One of the most heinous sins is they offered their children to idols as sacrifices. They built high places to Baal. The valley outside the east gate will become a valley of slaughter and death. God will make an example of His chosen people. This once proud, mighty nation will become an object of derision and humiliation. The world will view Israel and wag their head at a nation who was foolish and sinful. The calamity will be so bad people will eat their own children. This was fulfilled in the siege of 586 BC at the invasion by Nebuchadnezzar, and also in 70 AD when Titus the Roman general invaded Jerusalem. It was a poignant sermon. Jeremiah stood with broken pieces all around his feet and proclaimed their houses will lie in ruins as well. This judgment is the result of the people not hearing the words of the Lord. Add to this illustrated sermon the symbolism of the valley of Tophet which represents the place of garbage and burning, and God has made His point prophetically and poignantly. The vessel chosen was one used to store honey. The context of the passage infers this. Judah had lost her sweetness in the palate of God, and was being spewed out of the mouth of God.

Chapter 20

20.1-6 Now Pashur the son of Immer the priest, who was also chief governor in the house of the Lord, heard that Jeremiah prophesied these things. 2 Then Pashur smote Jeremiah the prophet, and put him in the stocks that were in the high gate of Benjamin, which was by the house of the Lord. 3 And it came to pass on the morrow, that Pashur brought forth Jeremiah out of the stocks. Then said Jeremiah unto him, The Lord hath not called thy name Pashur, but Magormissabib. 4 For thus saith the Lord, Behold, I will make thee a terror to thyself, and to all thy friends: and they shall fall by the sword of their enemies, and thine eyes shall behold it: and I will give all Judah into the hand of the king of Babylon, and he shall carry them captive into Babylon, and shall slay them with the sword. 5 Moreover I will deliver all the strength of this city, and all the labours thereof, and all the precious things thereof, and all the treasures of the kings of Judah will I give into the hand of their enemies, which shall spoil them, and take them, and carry them to Babylon. 6 And thou, Pashur, and all that dwell in thine house shall go into captivity: and thou shalt come to Babylon, and there thou shalt die, and shalt be buried there, thou, and all thy friends, to whom thou hast prophesied lies.

20.1-6 Jeremiah's dark days. When the authorities heard the sermon of the broken bottle, they beat Jeremiah and put him in the stocks overnight. Jeremiah had preached this sermon in the temple court and as the officers of the temple they were greatly offended. This incarceration included great pain from not being free to move for many hours. It was a method of torture. Upon his release, Jeremiah announces the verdict of judgment against Pashur, the temple officer, for his wrongful arrest and torture.

20.7-9 O Lord, thou hast deceived me, and I was deceived; thou art stronger than I, and hast prevailed: I am in derision daily, every one mocketh me. 8 For since I spake, I cried out, I cried violence and spoil; because the word of the Lord was made a reproach unto me, and a derision, daily. 9 Then I said, I will not make mention of him, nor speak any more in his name. But his word was in mine heart as a burning fire shut up in my bones, and I was weary with forbearing, and I could not stay.

20.7-9 Jeremiah deceived. This is such a strong accusation to anyone, but certainly when the one being accused is God Himself. The deep anguish and agony of Jeremiah overflows and he accuses God of deceiving him. The idea of being deceived here is Jeremiah was forced into this. He is saying God you made me do this. This is one of the moments we see the utter unhappiness of Jeremiah with his role as the mouthpiece of God. He is not doing his job willingly; he is being forced by God to execute the instructions. This is a window into his inner turmoil. Jeremiah feels God has overpowered him and seduced him to preach the sermon of the broken flask. This moment displays one of Jeremiah's most memorable moments. He confesses, he tried to stay quiet until he was weary with forbearing (to hold it in), but the word of God was like a fire shut up in his bones. Jeremiah feels like it is God who got him into this mess.

20.10-18 For I heard the defaming of many, fear on every side. Report, say they, and we will report it. All my familiars watched for my halting, saying, Peradventure he will be enticed, and we shall prevail against him, and we shall take our revenge on him. 11 But the Lord is with me as a mighty terrible one: therefore my persecutors shall stumble, and they shall not prevail: they shall be greatly ashamed; for they shall not prosper: their everlasting confusion shall never be forgotten. 12 But, O Lord of hosts, that triest the righteous, and seest the reins and the heart, let me see thy vengeance on them: for unto thee have I opened my cause. 13 Sing unto the Lord, praise ye the Lord: for he hath delivered the soul of the poor from the hand of evildoers. 14 Cursed be the day wherein I was born: let not the day wherein my mother bare me be blessed. 15 Cursed be the man who brought tidings to my father, saying, A man child is born unto thee; making him very glad. 16 And let that man be as the cities which the Lord overthrew, and repented not: and let him hear the cry in the morning, and the shouting at noontide; 17 Because he slew me not from the womb; or that my mother might have been my grave, and her womb to be always great with me. 18 Wherefore came I forth out of the womb to see labour and sorrow, that my days should be consumed with shame?

20.10-18 Jeremiah's disclaimer. It is human nature to defend one's self. To put the blame on others is common to all mankind. This is a rare instance where a man is putting the blame and onus of responsibility on God. Jeremiah is suffering for something he is not responsible for, and he is not shy about complaining. He begins by praying (10-12), then he sings (13) and gives God praise, but cannot avoid dissolving into self pity (14-18). The emotional pendulum has swung from compassion for the sinful people to depression and despair for his own personal calling as a mouthpiece of God. Jeremiah curses the day he was born. He curses the man who brought news of his birth. He questions why in the world was he even born. The amazing moment here is the honestly and transparency of Jeremiah. This was not written by his adversary. These words he wrote himself. Then God accepted his words, and wrote them down for the generations to come. They are part of the word that will never pass away. Serving God is not always easy. At times you may be overwhelmed. You also may wonder why you were ever born. We may never solve the riddle of our life, but we are indebted to this prophet for showing us we all fight similar battles and inner struggles.

Chapter 21

21.1-7 The word which came unto Jeremiah from the Lord, when king Zedekiah sent unto him Pashur the son of Melchiah, and Zephaniah the son of Maaseiah the priest, saying, 2 Enquire, I pray thee, of the Lord for us; for Nebuchadrezzar king of Babylon maketh war against us; if so be that the Lord will deal with us according to all his wondrous works, that he may go up from us. 3 Then said Jeremiah unto them, Thus shall ye say to Zedekiah: 4 Thus saith the Lord God of Israel; Behold, I will turn back the weapons of war that are in your hands, wherewith ye fight against the king of Babylon, and against the Chaldeans, which besiege you without the walls, and I will assemble them into the midst of this city. 5 And I myself will fight against you with an outstretched hand and with a strong arm, even in anger, and in fury, and in great wrath. 6 And I will smite the inhabitants of this city, both man and beast: they shall die of a great pestilence. 7 And afterward, saith the Lord, I will deliver Zedekiah king of Judah, and his servants, and the people, and such as are left in this city from the pestilence, from the sword, and from the famine, into the hand of Nebuchadrezzar king of Babylon, and into the hand of their enemies, and into the hand of those that seek their life: and he shall smite them with the edge of the sword; he shall not spare them, neither have pity, nor have mercy.

21.1-7 Zedekiah. This chapter is an illustration of the uniqueness of Jeremiah's writings. This chapter is about Zedekiah and later there will be chapters about kings who ruled before Zedekiah. The king is being attacked and he wants Jeremiah to assure him of good news. The news from God is not good. It is the worst news possible. Not only will God not help them, but God himself will fight against them. This section of Jeremiah's prophecy includes chapters 21-33. Chapters 21-29 are the details of the invasion by Babylon and chapters 30-33 are about the coming restoration. This lets us know God has the future in His control.

21.8-10 And unto this people thou shalt say, Thus saith the Lord; Behold, I set before you the way of life, and the way of death. 9 He that abideth in this city shall die by the sword, and by the famine, and by the pestilence: but he that goeth out, and falleth to the Chaldeans that besiege you, he shall live, and his life shall be unto him for a prey. 10 For I have set my face against this city for evil, and not for good, saith the Lord: it shall be given into the hand of the king of Babylon, and he shall burn it with fire.

21.8-10 God's patience. God is still patiently working with the people. People are living and dying, babies are being born as we look at the big picture overall. Their only hope is to leave the city, for the people who stay will fall by the sword.

21.11-14 And touching the house of the king of Judah, say, Hear ye the word of the Lord; 12 O house of David,

thus saith the Lord; Execute judgment in the morning, and deliver him that is spoiled out of the hand of the oppressor, lest my fury go out like fire, and burn that none can quench it, because of the evil of your doings. 13 Behold, I am against thee, O inhabitant of the valley, and rock of the plain, saith the Lord; which say, Who shall come down against us? or who shall enter into our habitations? 14 But I will punish you according to the fruit of your doings, saith the Lord: and I will kindle a fire in the forest thereof, and it shall devour all things round about it.

21.11-14 The house of David. David's towering influence is staggering. He has been dead for about 400 years yet God is still making decisions and judgments based on David. God has decided to make his glory known not in deliverance but in chastisement. There are dark days ahead for Jerusalem and it's inhabitants. The loving kindness of God is on display because He gives them guidance how to survive the coming disasters.

Chapter 22

22.1-10 Thus saith the Lord; Go down to the house of the king of Judah, and speak there this word, 2 And say, Hear the word of the Lord, O king of Judah, that sittest upon the throne of David, thou, and thy servants, and thy people that enter in by these gates: 3 Thus saith the Lord; Execute ye judgment and righteousness, and deliver the spoiled out of the hand of the oppressor: and do no wrong, do no violence to the stranger, the fatherless, nor the widow, neither shed innocent blood in this place. 4 For if ye do this thing indeed, then shall there enter in by the gates of this house kings sitting upon the throne of David, riding in chariots and on horses, he, and his servants, and his people. 5 But if ye will not hear these words, I swear by myself, saith the Lord, that this house shall become a desolation. 6 For thus saith the Lord unto the king's house of Judah; Thou art Gilead unto me, and the head of Lebanon: yet surely I will make thee a wilderness, and cities which are not inhabited. 7 And I will prepare destroyers against thee, every one with his weapons: and they shall cut down thy choice cedars, and cast them into the fire. 8 And many nations shall pass by this city, and they shall say every man to his neighbour, Wherefore hath the Lord done thus unto this great city? 9 Then they shall answer, Because they have forsaken the covenant of the Lord their God, and worshipped other gods, and served them. 10 Weep ye not for the dead, neither bemoan him: but weep sore for him that goeth away: for he shall return no more, nor see his native country.

22.1-10 If you are not aware that these chapters jump back and forth you will be easily confused. This was also a message to a king's household. That is the grouping here. This chapter begins by stating the opposite of what the previous chapter stated. This chapter is saying there is still a hope of mercy. This chapter was at an earlier time when the situation had not progressed as far. This is not waffling on the part of God or Jeremiah, these chapters should be considered independently and free standing.

22.11-17 For thus saith the Lord touching Shallum the son of Josiah king of Judah, which reigned instead of Josiah his father, which went forth out of this place; He shall not return thither any more: 12 But he shall die in the place whither they have led him captive, and shall see this land no more. 13 Woe unto him that buildeth his house by unrighteousness, and his chambers by wrong; that useth his neighbour's service without wages, and giveth him not for his work; 14 That saith, I will build me a wide house and large chambers, and cutteth him out windows; and it is cieled with cedar, and painted with vermilion. 15 Shalt thou reign, because thou closest thyself in cedar? did not thy father eat and drink, and do judgment and justice, and then it was well with him? 16 He judged the cause of the poor and needy; then it was well with him: was not this to know me? saith the Lord. 17 But thine eyes and thine heart are not but for thy covetousness, and for to shed innocent blood, and for oppression, and for violence, to do it.

22.11-17 The issues here are the same as those Amos spoke to the Northern Kingdom about. There is injustice, luxury, covetousness, rape and murder. This causes Jeremiah to proclaim Jehoiakim will die unlamented and unmourned. Jehoiakim did in fact die in ignominy (36.30-31). As these social issues and inhumane treatment to fellow man brought down the Northern Kingdom, it will also bring down Judah.

22.18-30 Therefore thus saith the Lord concerning Jehoiakim the son of Josiah king of Judah; They shall not lament for him, saying, Ah my brother! or, Ah sister! they shall not lament for him, saying, Ah lord! or, Ah his glory! 19 He shall be buried with the burial of an ass, drawn and cast forth beyond the gates of Jerusalem. 20 Go up to Lebanon, and cry; and lift up thy voice in Bashan, and cry from the passages: for all thy lovers are destroyed. 21 I spake unto thee in thy prosperity; but thou saidst, I will not hear. This hath been thy manner from thy youth, that thou obeyedst not my voice. 22 The wind shall eat up all thy pastors, and thy lovers shall go into captivity: surely then shalt thou be ashamed and confounded for all thy wickedness. 23 O inhabitant of Lebanon, that makest thy nest in the cedars, how gracious shalt thou be when pangs come upon thee, the pain as of a woman in travail! 24 As I live, saith the Lord, though Coniah the son of Jehoiakim king of Judah were the signet upon my right hand, yet would I pluck thee thence; 25 And I will give thee into the hand of them that seek thy life, and into the hand of them whose face thou fearest, even into the hand of Nebuchadrezzar king of Babylon, and into the hand of the Chaldeans. 26 And I will cast thee out, and thy mother that bare thee, into another country, where ye were not born; and there shall ye die. 27 But to the land whereunto they desire to return, thither shall they not

return. 28 Is this man Coniah a despised broken idol? is he a vessel wherein is no pleasure? wherefore are they cast out, he and his seed, and are cast into a land which they know not? 29 O earth, earth, earth, hear the word of the Lord. 30 Thus saith the Lord, Write ye this man childless, a man that shall not prosper in his days: for no man of his seed shall prosper, sitting upon the throne of David, and ruling any more in Judah.

22.18-30 The people of the land are called upon to mourn and lament. Their kings are being carried captive and delivered to the king of Babylon. They are threatened with exile in a strange country. They are told they will die there without children. There is an inference the line of Solomon will cease. None of Jehoiachin's seven children became king. In Matt 1.18 Joseph, the husband of Mary is of the line of Jehoichin. Because Jesus was born of a virgin, this means the pronouncement against Jehoichin is not contradicted. Jehoichin's grandson Zerubbabel was governor of Judah, but never a king. The kingship of Israel and Judah ended with the 6th century BC. Jesus' human descent is traced through Nathan, the brother of Solomon on his mother's side. Jesus is heir to David's throne on both sides of his parents. Christ did not abrogate the prophetic curse on Jehoiachin's line. This demonstrates the accuracy of the scriptures.

Chapter 23

23.1 Woe be unto the pastors that destroy and scatter the sheep of my pasture! saith the Lord.

23.1 False prophets. Jeremiah addresses one of the most harmful issues of Judah's sordid failure. The issue is false prophets. This is a recurring problem in Judah's history and will continue into the New Testament. Why are these false prophets so effective while true prophets struggle for an audience? It is because these false prophets speak what the people want to hear. They are people pleasers. They love the praise of men and being accepted. No prophet in the Bible is more the antithesis of this than Jeremiah. Jeremiah spoke the word of God faithfully. When his message was offensive and unwanted he still spoke it as God directed. This is the mark of a true prophet. They belong to God and answer only to him. Anything less and the prophet becomes a hireling.

23.2-8 Therefore thus saith the Lord God of Israel against the pastors that feed my people; Ye have scattered my flock, and driven them away, and have not visited them: behold, I will visit upon you the evil of your doings, saith the Lord. 3 And I will gather the remnant of my flock out of all countries whither I have

driven them, and will bring them again to their folds; and they shall be fruitful and increase. 4 And I will set up shepherds over them which shall feed them: and they shall fear no more, nor be dismayed, neither shall they be lacking, saith the Lord. 5 Behold, the days come, saith the Lord, that I will raise unto David a righteous Branch, and a King shall reign and prosper, and shall execute judgment and justice in the earth. 6 In his days Judah shall be saved, and Israel shall dwell safely: and this is his name whereby he shall be called, The Lord Our Righteousness. 7 Therefore, behold, the days come, saith the Lord, that they shall no more say, The Lord liveth, which brought up the children of Israel out of the land of Egypt; 8 But, The Lord liveth, which brought up and which led the seed of the house of Israel out of the north country, and from all countries whither I had driven them; and they shall dwell in their own land.

23.2-8 Pastors are shepherds. The word pastor here (raah) means to tend a flock. The idea here is the spiritual leader. These shepherds did not faithfully lead the flock, but instead scattered (dashed in pieces) them. What a travesty of their calling. This is still true today in many of the celebrity, television religious leaders who are people pleasers. They are not faithful shepherds. God is promising He will provide them with faithful shepherds. The prophecy goes further and includes the coming of the branch of David, which is Christ. He is called Jehovah tsedeq (The Lord our Righteousness). This prophecy does foretell the first coming of Jesus Christ, but it also has prophetical implications of when Jesus will return and become the King of Kings of all the earth in His millennial reign of 1000 years. This regathering of God's people will include gathering his flock from all countries of the earth.

23.9-32 Mine heart within me is broken because of the prophets; all my bones shake; I am like a drunken man, and like a man whom wine hath overcome, because of the Lord, and because of the words of his holiness. 10 For the land is full of adulterers; for because of swearing the land mourneth; the pleasant places of the wilderness are dried up, and their course is evil, and their force is not right. 11 For both prophet and priest are profane; yea, in my house have I found their wickedness, saith the Lord. 12 Wherefore their way shall be unto them as slippery ways in the darkness: they shall be driven on, and fall therein: for I will bring evil upon them, even the year of their visitation, saith the Lord. 13 And I have seen folly in the prophets of Samaria; they prophesied in Baal, and caused my people Israel to err. 14 I have seen also in the prophets of Jerusalem an horrible thing: they commit adultery, and walk in lies: they strengthen also the hands of evildoers, that none doth return from his wickedness; they are all of them unto me as Sodom, and the inhabitants thereof as Gomorrah. 15 Therefore thus saith the Lord of hosts concerning the prophets; Behold, I will feed them with wormwood, and make them drink the water of gall: for from the prophets of Jerusalem is profaneness gone forth into all the land. 16 Thus saith the Lord of hosts, Hearken not unto the words of the prophets that prophesy unto you: they make you vain: they speak a vision of their own heart, and not out of the mouth of the Lord. 17 They say still unto them that despise me, The Lord hath said, Ye shall have peace; and they say unto every one that walketh after the imagination of his own heart, No evil shall come upon you. 18 For who hath stood in the counsel of the Lord, and hath perceived and heard his word? who hath marked his word, and heard it? 19 Behold, a whirlwind of the Lord is gone forth in fury, even a grievous whirlwind: it shall fall grievously upon the head of the wicked. 20 The anger of the Lord shall not return, until he have executed, and till he have performed the thoughts of his heart: in the latter days ye shall consider it perfectly. 21 I have not sent these prophets, yet they ran: I have not spoken to them, yet they prophesied. 22 But if they had stood in my counsel, and had caused my people to hear my words, then they should have turned them from their evil way, and from the evil of their doings. 23 Am I a God at hand, saith the Lord, and not a God afar off? 24 Can any hide himself in secret places that I shall not see him? saith the Lord. Do not I fill heaven and earth? saith the Lord. 25 I have heard what the prophets said, that prophesy lies in my name, saying, I have dreamed, I have dreamed. 26 How long shall this be in the heart of the prophets that prophesy lies? yea, they are prophets of the deceit of their own heart; 27 Which think to cause my people to forget my name by their dreams which they tell every man to his neighbour, as their fathers have forgotten my name for Baal. 28 The prophet that hath a dream, let him tell a dream; and he that hath my word, let him speak my word faithfully. What is the chaff to the wheat? saith the Lord. 29 Is not my word like as a fire? saith the Lord; and like a hammer that breaketh the rock in pieces? 30 Therefore, behold, I am against the prophets, saith the Lord, that steal my words every one from his neighbour. 31 Behold, I am against the prophets, saith the Lord, that use their tongues, and say, He saith. 32 Behold, I am against them that prophesy false dreams, saith the Lord, and do tell them, and cause my people to err by their lies, and by their lightness; yet I sent them not, nor commanded them: therefore they shall not profit this people at all, saith the Lord.

23.9-32 The contrast. Jeremiah turns his eye from the coming of the Great Shepherd, Jesus Christ, to those around him who are liars in the disguise of the prophetical mantle. This moment is so impacting he literally feels sick and dizzy. He begins to catalog their long sordid history. Jeremiah is cataloging centuries of false prophets. Their actions are beyond horrible. They lie, they strengthen the hands of evildoers, they reek of Sodom and Gomorrah, which is always a type of the lowest level humanity can sink. He announces how God will deal with these false prophets. They will take bitterness into themselves. Jeremiah pleads with the people to not listen to these liars. They are dishonest. They tell the very people whom God is displeased with they shall have peace. No evil is coming your way, and the people believe them. God clearly disowns any part of these prophets. He did not send them. These prophets claim dreams from God but these dreams are contrary to the revealed word of God. This always identifies a false prophet. His words must match the Word. When the dream is not in synch with the Word, the dream is false and self-willed. God calls these shallow prophets chaff and the wind of His fury will carry them away. God is against these prophets. The ultimate conclusion is these prophets do not profit the people at all. Modern day preachers who make people feel empowered and confident and do not preach the word as it is written, are the offspring of these false prophets six centuries before Christ.

23.33-40 And when this people, or the prophet, or a priest, shall ask thee, saying, What is the burden of the Lord? thou shalt then say unto them, What burden? I will even forsake you, saith the Lord. 34 And as for the prophet, and the priest, and the people, that shall say, The burden of the Lord, I will even punish that man and his house.

35 Thus shall ye say every one to his neighbour, and every one to his brother, What hath the Lord answered? and, What hath the Lord spoken? 36 And the burden of the Lord shall ye mention no more: for every man's word shall be his burden; for ye have perverted the words of the living God, of the Lord of hosts our God. 37 Thus shalt thou say to the prophet, What hath the Lord answered thee? and, What hath the Lord spoken? 38 But since ye say, The burden of the Lord; therefore thus saith the Lord; Because ye say this word, The burden of the Lord, and I have sent unto you, saying, Ye shall not say, The burden of the Lord; 39 Therefore, behold, I, even I, will utterly forget you, and I will forsake you, and the city that I gave you and your fathers, and cast you out of my presence: 40 And I will bring an everlasting reproach upon you, and a perpetual shame, which shall not be forgotten.

23.33-40 The refrain to false prophets. When these liars ask Jeremiah what the burden (utterance), of the Lord is, Jeremiah is instructed to remain silent. This reflects in the actions of Jeremiah, that God does not speak to these prophets so why should Jeremiah? To any watching this exchange, Jeremiah again shows in living color God's attitude toward these perverters of the Word. Jeremiah's parting shot is that God will bring an everlasting, perpetual shame on these liars. The idea is a vanishing line on the horizon with no end. Such is the shame of any who pervert the words of God and speak false dreams of self-aggrandizement.

Chapter 24

24.1-10 The Lord shewed me, and, behold, two baskets of figs were set before the temple of the Lord, after that Nebuchadrezzar king of Babylon had carried away captive Jeconiah the son of Jehoiakim king of Judah, and the princes of Judah, with the carpenters and smiths, from Jerusalem, and had brought them to Babylon. 2 One basket had very good figs, even like the figs that are first ripe: and the other basket had very naughty figs, which could not be eaten, they were so bad. 3 Then said the Lord unto me, What seest thou, Jeremiah? And I said, Figs; the good figs, very good; and the evil, very evil, that cannot be eaten, they are so evil. 4 Again the word of the Lord came unto me, saying, 5 Thus saith the Lord, the God of Israel; Like these good figs, so will I acknowledge them that are carried away captive of Judah, whom I have sent out of this place into the land of the Chaldeans for their good. 6 For I will set mine eyes upon them for good, and I will bring them again to this land: and I will build them, and not pull them down; and I will plant them, and not pluck them up. 7 And I will give them an heart to know me, that I am the Lord: and they shall be my people, and I will be their God: for they shall return unto me with their whole heart. 8 And as the evil figs, which cannot be eaten, they are so evil; surely thus saith the Lord, So will I give Zedekiah the king of Judah, and his princes, and the residue of Jerusalem, that remain in this land, and them that dwell in the land of Egypt: 9 And I will deliver them to be removed into all the kingdoms of the earth for their hurt, to be a reproach and a proverb, a taunt and a curse, in all places whither I shall drive them. 10 And I will send the sword, the famine, and the pestilence, among them, till they be consumed from off the land that I gave unto them and to their fathers.

24.1-10 The parable of the figs. The explication in this parable is an everlasting principal to God. Earliest man recognized this. Abraham, one of the earliest men in the Bible said "shall not the God of the earth do right?" (Gen 18.25). Abraham appealed unto God in behalf of Sodom. The appeal was based on would God destroy the righteous with the wicked. God has a principal of separation. The good figs will be separated from the naughty (bad or evil) figs. This concept is universal and eternal. Jesus promised to throughly purge his floor of the wheat and the chaff (Matt 3.12). In this analogy the good figs represent the people who will return and be restored to the land. This is God saying they are good on the inside. The bad figs represent the incorrigible people who have been obdurate and resisted the words of the true prophet Jeremiah. Their future is shame, hurt, taunts, and curses. Then their eventual destiny is sword, famine, and pestilence. As bad figs are thrown away, so God gives these people up to ignominious ruin.

Chapter 25

25.1-14 The word that came to Jeremiah concerning all the people of Judah in the fourth year of Jehoiakim the son of Josiah king of Judah, that was the first year of Nebuchadrezzar king of Babylon; 2 The which Jeremiah the prophet spake unto all the people of Judah, and to all the inhabitants of Jerusalem, saying, 3 From the thirteenth year of Josiah the son of Amon king of Judah, even unto this day, that is the three and twentieth year, the word of the Lord hath come unto me, and I have spoken unto you, rising early and speaking; but ye have not hearkened. 4 And the Lord hath sent unto you all his servants the prophets, rising early and sending them; but ye have not hearkened, nor inclined your ear to hear. 5 They said, Turn ye again now every one from his evil way, and from the evil of your doings, and dwell in the land that the Lord hath given unto you and to your fathers for ever and ever: 6 And go not after other gods to serve them, and to worship them, and provoke me not to anger with the works of your hands; and I will do you no hurt. 7 Yet ye have not hearkened unto me, saith the Lord; that ye might provoke me to anger with the works of your hands to your own hurt. 8 Therefore thus saith the Lord of hosts; Because ye have not heard my words, 9 Behold, I will send and take all the families of the north, saith the Lord, and Nebuchadrezzar the king of Babylon, my servant, and will bring them against this land, and against the inhabitants thereof, and against all these nations round about, and will utterly destroy them, and make them an astonishment, and an hissing, and perpetual desolations. 10 Moreover I will take from them the voice of mirth, and the voice of gladness, the voice of the bridegroom, and the voice of the bride, the sound of the millstones, and the light of the candle. 11 And this whole land shall be a desolation, and an astonishment; and these nations shall serve the king of Babylon seventy years. 12 And it shall come to pass, when seventy years are accomplished, that I will punish the king of Babylon, and that nation, saith the Lord, for their iniquity, and the land of the Chaldeans, and will make it perpetual desolations. 13 And I will bring upon that land all my words which I have pronounced against it, even all that is written in this book, which Jeremiah hath prophesied against all the nations. 14 For many nations and great kings shall serve themselves of them also: and I will recompense them according to their deeds, and according to the works of their own hands.

25.1-14 The 70 years. Jeremiah has now been speaking for 10 years to the people, and he is about to deliver one of the most important pieces of information in the Bible. This begins the second half of the book of Jeremiah. Jeremiah again documents the many times God has tried to reach out to this hardhearted people. They were pleaded with to leave the false Gods and false prophets. They have not listened or complied. Jeremiah again states the coming invasion will be from the North by Nebuchadnezzar. This will be a time of great sadness and horror. Then Jeremiah sounds the alarm that rings with such import. It will be for 70 years. This is an important time element and is the subject of much debate. The prophet Daniel will also pick up this refrain and define it further (Daniel chapter 9). It will become the timeline for the nation of Israel and for God's future plans for the entire globe. As chemotherapy is to a cancer patient, so this 70 years of captivity will be to the nation of Israel. This captivity will kill off things that have beset the nation for centuries and that have slowly taken the lifeblood of the nation. Idolatry will be cured in the 70 years. The problem of false prophets seems to be universally overcome. The rise of synagogues and scribes have their birth in this time of captivity. This time is a rebirth of sorts of the nation. When the forty two thousand plus people return in the repatriation, it is a different nation from that moment forward. The nation of Israel is never the same. The problems of 1000 years that could not be overcome are jettisoned forever. The exodus from Egypt with it's lingering effects, the dissuasion of the Judges is smoothed out, and the failures of the Monarchy are finally mended. In the grand scheme of time, no period in the Bible is of greater import than this 70 years of captivity. This time began with the fall of Jerusalem in 586 BC and lasted until 516 BC when the temple is rebuilt by the exiles.

25.15-38 For thus saith the Lord God of Israel unto me; Take the wine cup of this fury at my hand, and cause all the nations, to whom I send thee, to drink it. 16 And they shall drink, and be moved, and be mad, because of the sword that I will send among them. 17 Then took I the cup at the Lord's hand, and made all the nations to drink, unto whom the Lord had sent me: 18 To wit, Jerusalem, and the cities of Judah, and the kings thereof, and the princes thereof, to make them a desolation, an astonishment, an hissing, and a curse; as it is this day; 19 Pharaoh king of Egypt, and his servants, and his princes, and all his people; 20 And all the mingled people, and

all the kings of the land of Uz, and all the kings of the land of the Philistines, and Ashkelon, and Azzah, and Ekron, and the remnant of Ashdod, 21 Edom, and Moab, and the children of Ammon, 22 And all the kings of Tyrus, and all the kings of Zidon, and the kings of the isles which are beyond the sea, 23 Dedan, and Tema, and Buz, and all that are in the utmost corners, 24 And all the kings of Arabia, and all the kings of the mingled people that dwell in the desert, 25 And all the kings of Zimri, and all the kings of Elam, and all the kings of the Medes, 26 And all the kings of the north, far and near, one with another, and all the kingdoms of the world, which are upon the face of the earth: and the king of Sheshach shall drink after them. 27 Therefore thou shalt say unto them, Thus saith the Lord of hosts, the God of Israel; Drink ye, and be drunken, and spue, and fall, and rise no more, because of the sword which I will send among you. 28 And it shall be, if they refuse to take the cup at thine hand to drink, then shalt thou say unto them, Thus saith the Lord of hosts; Ye shall certainly drink. 29 For, lo, I begin to bring evil on the city which is called by my name, and should ye be utterly unpunished? Ye shall not be unpunished: for I will call for a sword upon all the inhabitants of the earth, saith the Lord of hosts. 30 Therefore prophesy thou against them all these words, and say unto them, The Lord shall roar from on high, and utter his voice from his holy habitation; he shall mightily roar upon his habitation; he shall give a shout, as they that tread the grapes, against all the inhabitants of the earth. 31 A noise shall come even to the ends of the earth; for the Lord hath a controversy with the nations, he will plead with all flesh; he will give them that are wicked to the sword, saith the Lord. 32 Thus saith the Lord of hosts, Behold, evil shall go forth from nation to nation, and a great whirlwind shall be raised up from the coasts of the earth. 33 And the slain of the Lord shall be at that day from one end of the earth even unto the other end of the earth: they shall not be lamented, neither gathered, nor buried; they shall be dung upon the ground. 34 Howl, ye shepherds, and cry; and wallow yourselves in the ashes, ye principal of the flock: for the days of your slaughter and of your dispersions are accomplished; and ye shall fall like a pleasant vessel. 35 And the shepherds shall have no way to flee, nor the principal of the flock to escape. 36 A voice of the cry of the shepherds, and an howling of the principal of the flock, shall be heard: for the Lord hath spoiled their pasture. 37 And the peaceable habitations are cut down because of the fierce anger of the Lord. 38 He hath forsaken his covert, as the lion: for their land is desolate because of the fierceness of the oppressor, and because of his fierce anger.

25.15-38 The cup of wrath. The eye of the prophet now gazes worldwide and takes in all the nations. Here in chapter 25 he begins the second half of his book. The first 24 chapters document the sins of Judah and the failures of Israel. God is not just concerned with Israel and Judah, but God is working to bring all the earth to an expected end. The rest of his book now deals with the nations of the world primarily. The cup is a symbol of divine judgment. Jesus drank the cup in the garden when he was taking in the divine wrath against all the sin of humanity. The cup is mentioned 4 times in the book of Revelation. The cup is used in the communion service as well. It is an important symbol that represents taking issues to heart. Jeremiah foreshadows the moment when Jesus will take the cup for the world's sins. The cup of judgment here is also about the nations of the world. So much of Jeremiah's interaction with God, and with others, reflects the larger more encompassing actions of Jesus when he comes. There is a triad sequence of the cup. It is drink, then stagger, and finally go mad. This sequel will happen to planet earth. Earth will drink of the cup, then earth will stagger at the judgments of God, and finally planet earth will go mad.

Chapter 26

26.1-9 In the beginning of the reign of Jehoiakim the son of Josiah king of Judah came this word from the Lord, saying, 2 Thus saith the Lord; Stand in the court of the Lord's house, and speak unto all the cities of Judah, which come to worship in the Lord's house, all the words that I command thee to speak unto them; diminish not a word: 3 If so be they will hearken, and turn every man from his evil way, that I may repent me of the evil, which I purpose to do unto them because of the evil of their doings. 4 And thou shalt say unto them, Thus saith the Lord; If ye will not hearken to me, to walk in my law, which I have set before you, 5 To hearken to the words of my servants the prophets, whom I sent unto you, both rising up early, and sending them, but ye have not hearkened; 6 Then will I make this house like Shiloh, and will make this city a curse to all the nations of the earth.7 So the priests and the prophets and all the people heard Jeremiah speaking these words in the house of the Lord. 8 Now it came to pass, when Jeremiah had made an end of speaking all that the Lord had commanded him to speak unto all the people, that the priests and the prophets and all the people took him, saying, Thou shalt surely die. 9 Why hast thou prophesied in the name of the Lord, saying, This house shall be like Shiloh, and this city shall be desolate without an inhabitant? And all the people were gathered against Jeremiah in the house of the Lord.

26.1-9 Death threats. Few preachers will ever face the animosity Jeremiah faced. When Jeremiah spoke this sermon to them, their reaction was, they decided to kill him. What causes this kind of passion to run so deep? It is understood for them to be offended or even disagree, but kill someone for a sermon? Jeremiah was speaking against their false reliance on the temple itself and the corrupt priesthood. This was later seen in the inquisition as well. Men were burned at the stake for their beliefs. Some modern religions foster this practice as well. Radical groups today sometimes murder and decapitate people who dissent. The passions of religion run deep in mankind.

26.10-15 When the princes of Judah heard these things, then they came up from the king's house unto the house of the Lord, and sat down in the entry of the new gate of the Lord's house. 11 Then spake the priests and the prophets unto the princes and to all the people, saying, This man is worthy to die; for he hath prophesied against this city, as ye have heard with your ears. 12 Then spake Jeremiah unto all the princes and to all the people, saying, The Lord sent me to prophesy against this house and against this city all the words that ye have heard. 13 Therefore now amend your ways and your doings, and obey the voice of the Lord your God; and the Lord will repent him of the evil that he hath pronounced against you. 14 As for me, behold, I am in your hand: do with me as seemeth good and meet unto you. 15 But know ye for certain, that if ye put me to death, ye shall surely bring innocent blood upon yourselves, and upon this city, and upon the inhabitants thereof:

for of a truth the Lord hath sent me unto you to speak all these words in your ears.

26.10-15 The officials. The people are joined by the officials in the verdict of death. It would seem reasonable that these leaders of men would advise caution or restraint. These wicked leaders do not show restraint. These rulers mirror the vindictiveness of the common people. Jeremiah shows great grace in not resisting. He does warn his death would indict the city of shedding innocent blood. This was considered egregious and heinous in Israel. In fact, Jeremiah was attacking the very root of the problem: a corrupt officialdom and priesthood. This was the real controversy God had with Judah.

26.16-24 Then said the princes and all the people unto the priests and to the prophets; This man is not worthy to die: for he hath spoken to us in the name of the Lord our God. 17 Then rose up certain of the elders of the land, and spake to all the assembly of the people, saying, 18 Micah the Morasthite prophesied in the days of Hezekiah king of Judah, and spake to all the people of Judah, saying, Thus saith the Lord of hosts; Zion shall be plowed like a field, and Jerusalem shall become heaps, and the mountain of the house as the high places of a forest. 19 Did Hezekiah king of Judah and all Judah put him at all to death? did he not fear the Lord, and besought the Lord, and the Lord repented him of the evil which he had pronounced against them? Thus might we procure great evil against our souls. 20 And there was also a man that prophesied in the name of the Lord, Urijah the son of Shemaiah of Kirjathjearim, who prophesied against this city and against this land according to all the words of Jeremiah. 21 And when Jehoiakim the king, with all his mighty men, and all the princes, heard his words,

the king sought to put him to death: but when Urijah heard it, he was afraid, and fled, and went into Egypt; 22 And Jehoiakim the king sent men into Egypt, namely, Elnathan the son of Achbor, and certain men with him into Egypt. 23 And they fetched forth Urijah out of Egypt, and brought him unto Jehoiakim the king; who slew him with the sword, and cast his dead body into the graves of the common people. 24 Nevertheless the hand of Ahikam the son of Shaphan was with Jeremiah, that they should not give him into the hand of the people to put him to death.

26.16-24 Micah and Urijah. The leaders attempt to justify their death request. Like lawyers before a Supreme Court they present past cases and sentences. The sentence passed upon Micah during the days of Hezekiah is presented, even though Micah was not killed. Then the sentence and resulting death of Urijah is presented as viable reason to indict and execute Jeremiah. Jeremiah is represented by Ahikam. Ahikam had a long record of faithful service among the hierarchy of the nation. He was a member of the delegation sent by Josiah to the prophetess Huldah (2K22.12). Ahikam' son Gedaliah would later become the governor of Judah and be charged with the care of Jeremiah. (40.5). The high standing and respect of this man Ahikam keeps Jeremiah from being executed by this barbarous, degenerate populace. The princes and priests wanted to incite the general population to kill Jeremiah so as not to reap the fruit of the odious crime themselves. The parallel to Jesus is seen here again when the chief priests and elders seek to inflame the people to kill Jesus (Mt 27.20). Jeremiah's life is spared, but the population is still adverse to him.

Chapter 27

27.1-21 In the beginning of the reign of Jehoiakim the son of Josiah king of Judah came this word unto Jeremiah from the Lord, saying, 2 Thus saith the Lord to me; Make thee bonds and yokes, and put them upon thy neck, 3 And send them to the king of Edom, and to the king of Moab, and to the king of the Ammonites, and to the king of Tyrus, and to the king of Zidon, by the hand of the messengers which come to Jerusalem unto Zedekiah king of Judah; 4 And command them to say unto their masters, Thus saith the Lord of hosts, the God of Israel; Thus shall ye say unto your masters; 5 I have made the earth, the man and the beast that are upon the ground, by my great power and by my outstretched arm, and have given it unto whom it seemed meet unto me. 6 And now have I given all these lands into the hand of Nebuchadnezzar the king of Babylon, my servant; and the beasts of the field have I given him also to serve him. 7 And all nations shall serve him, and his son, and his son's son, until the very time of his land come: and then many nations and great kings shall serve themselves of him. 8 And it shall come to pass, that the nation and kingdom which will not serve the same Nebuchadnezzar the king of Babylon, and that will not put their neck under the yoke of the king of Babylon, that nation will

I punish, saith the Lord, with the sword, and with the famine, and with the pestilence, until I have consumed them by his hand. 9 Therefore hearken not ye to your prophets, nor to your diviners, nor to your dreamers, nor to your enchanters, nor to your sorcerers, which speak unto you, saying, Ye shall not serve the king of Babylon: 10 For they prophesy a lie unto you, to remove you far from your land; and that I should drive you out, and ye should perish. 11 But the nations that bring their neck under the yoke of the king of Babylon, and serve him, those will I let remain still in their own land, saith the Lord; and they shall till it, and dwell therein. 12 I spake also to Zedekiah king of Judah according to all these words, saying, Bring your necks under the yoke of the king of Babylon, and serve him and his people, and live. 13 Why will ye die, thou and thy people, by the sword, by the famine, and by the pestilence, as the Lord hath spoken against the nation that will not serve the king of Babylon? 14 Therefore hearken not unto the words of the prophets that speak unto you, saying, Ye shall not serve the king of Babylon: for they prophesy a lie unto you. 15 For I have not sent them, saith the Lord, yet they prophesy a lie in my name; that I might drive you out, and that ye might perish, ye, and the prophets that prophesy unto you. 16 Also I spake to the priests and to all this people, saying, Thus saith the Lord; Hearken not to the words of your prophets that prophesy unto you, saying, Behold, the vessels of the Lord's house shall now shortly be brought again from Babylon: for they prophesy a lie unto you. 17 Hearken not unto them; serve the king of Babylon, and live: wherefore should this city be laid waste? 18 But if they be prophets, and if the word of the Lord be with them, let them now make intercession to the Lord of hosts, that the vessels which are left in the house of the Lord, and in the house of the

king of Judah, and at Jerusalem, go not to Babylon. 19 For thus saith the Lord of hosts concerning the pillars, and concerning the sea, and concerning the bases, and concerning the residue of the vessels that remain in this city. 20 Which Nebuchadnezzar king of Babylon took not, when he carried away captive Jeconiah the son of Jehoiakim king of Judah from Jerusalem to Babylon, and all the nobles of Judah and Jerusalem; 21 Yea, thus saith the Lord of hosts, the God of Israel, concerning the vessels that remain in the house of the Lord, and in the house of the king of Judah and of Jerusalem;

27.1-21 Nebuchadnezzar's yoke. We see here one of the reasons Jeremiah is a major prophet. The scope and reach of the ministry of a major prophet is always large and includes many nations. The minor prophets were usually narrow in their field of ministry. God used major prophets to speak to the world at large not just to Israel and Judah. In this passage Jeremiah is instructed to inform the nations Edom, Moab, Ammon, Tyre and Zidon that God has chosen Nebuchadnezzar as his hand to execute judgment on these nations. Those nations that comply will be spared terrible war and mutilation. This shows God is always interested in the world at large and not just the nation of Judah. Jeremiah demonstrates this by a yoke that represents the yoke of Nebuchadnezzar. God further informs them it is futile to resist or listen to their false prophets.

27.22 They shall be carried to Babylon, and there shall they be until the day that I visit them, saith the Lord; then will I bring them up, and restore them to this place.

27.22 Zedekiah. Jeremiah shifts his words to the King of Judah in particular. The message is ditto to the message to the surrounding nations. Zedekiah is again remonstrated to ignore the words of prophets who prophesy deliverance. The appeal is to save the city itself so it will not be destroyed. There is a beautiful side note here when God reminds them the vessels of holy things will be taken to Babylon and preserved for the return in seventy years. Nebuchadnezzar left these valuable vessels when he took Jeconiah captive, but they will be preserved in Babylon just as the nation is preserved in. Babylon. The message loudly and vividly proclaimed here is God protects and preserves holy things and holy people.

Chapter 28

28.1-11 And it came to pass the same year, in the beginning of the reign of Zedekiah king of Judah, in the fourth year, and in the fifth month, that Hananiah the son of Azur the prophet, which was of Gibeon, spake unto me in the house of the Lord, in the presence of the priests and of all the people, saying, 2 Thus speaketh the Lord of hosts, the God of Israel, saying, I have broken the yoke of the king of Babylon. 3 Within two full years will I bring again into this place all the vessels of the Lord's house, that Nebuchadnezzar king of Babylon took away from this place, and carried them to Babylon: 4 And I will bring again to this place Jeconiah the son of Jehoiakim king of Judah, with all the captives of Judah, that went into Babylon, saith the Lord: for I will break the yoke of the king of Babylon. 5 Then the prophet Jeremiah said unto the prophet Hananiah in the presence of the priests, and in the presence of all the people that stood in the house of the Lord, 6 Even the prophet Jeremiah said, Amen: the Lord do so: the Lord perform thy words which thou hast prophesied, to bring again the vessels of the Lord's house, and all that is carried away captive, from Babylon into this place. 7 Nevertheless hear thou now this word that I speak in thine ears, and in the ears of all the people; 8 The prophets that have been before me and before thee of old prophesied both against many countries, and against great kingdoms, of war, and of evil, and of pestilence. 9 The prophet which prophesieth of peace, when the word of the prophet shall come to pass, then shall the prophet be known, that the Lord hath truly sent him. 10 Then Hananiah the prophet took the yoke from off the prophet Jeremiah's neck, and brake it. 11 And Hananiah spake in the presence of all the people, saying, Thus saith the Lord; Even so will I break the yoke of Nebuchadnezzar king of Babylon from the neck of all nations within the space of two full years. And the prophet Jeremiah went his way.

28.1-11. Hananiah. We have a snapshot view here of the false prophets, and their effect on the people, and their opposition to Jeremiah. This man is a son of a prophet and his credentials are as valid as those of Jeremiah. He refutes the entire prophecy of the yoke spoken by Jeremiah in the temple. Jeremiah still has the yoke on his neck and Hananiah takes it off Jeremiah and breaks the yoke. Hananiah attempts to fight fire with fire and use the same tactics God told Jeremiah to use. This sequence of attempts backfires on this false prophet, and ultimately Hananiah signs his own death certificate. With a great show of drama, Hananiah takes the yoke off Jeremiah and breaks it and boldly refutes Jeremiah's words and declares, in two years this yoke will be broken. God is an unseen member of the audience that day. Jeremiah simply walks away; again symbolizing what God's reaction is to this display of lies. God will not dignify their lies with a response.

28.12-17 Then the word of the Lord came unto Jeremiah the prophet, after that Hananiah the prophet had broken the yoke from off the neck of the prophet Jeremiah,

saying, 13 Go and tell Hananiah, saying, Thus saith the Lord; Thou hast broken the yokes of wood; but thou shalt make for them yokes of iron. 14 For thus saith the Lord of hosts, the God of Israel; I have put a yoke of iron upon the neck of all these nations, that they may serve Nebuchadnezzar king of Babylon; and they shall serve him: and I have given him the beasts of the field also. 15 Then said the prophet Jeremiah unto Hananiah the prophet, Hear now, Hananiah; The Lord hath not sent thee; but thou makest this people to trust in a lie. 16 Therefore thus saith the Lord; Behold, I will cast thee from off the face of the earth: this year thou shalt die, because thou hast taught rebellion against the Lord. 17 So Hananiah the prophet died the same year in the seventh month.

28.12-17 God's answer. God then tells his true prophet what will happen. Poetic justice is an art refined by God to a degree that is humanly impossible. God's answer is, Hananiah you have broken the yoke of wood and in doing so you have forged yokes of iron. In your attempt to break the yoke God ordained, you have inadvertently forged stronger yokes that are unbreakable. This is true poetic justice on a galactic scale. Jeremiah utters the death sentence on this mouthpiece of lies, Hananiah. Hananiah is informed that God did not send you, and you have made this people trust in a lie. Therefore you will die this year because you have taught rebellion against the Lord. This is the ministry of all false prophets, rebellion against God himself. The false prophet Hananiah died in the seventh month that year. We are again left to wonder why this people of Judah are immune to these staggering events that endorse Jeremiah. Jeremiah's words are fulfilled exactly, and Judah continues to speed helter-skelter down the road to captivity.

Chapter 29

29.1-14 Now these are the words of the letter that Jeremiah the prophet sent from Jerusalem unto the residue of the elders which were carried away captives, and to the priests, and to the prophets, and to all the people whom Nebuchadnezzar had carried away captive from Jerusalem to Babylon; 2 (After that Jeconiah the king, and the queen, and the eunuchs, the princes of Judah and Jerusalem, and the carpenters, and the smiths, were departed from Jerusalem;) 3 By the hand of Elasah the son of Shaphan, and Gemariah the son of Hilkiah, (whom Zedekiah king of Judah sent unto Babylon to Nebuchadnezzar king of Babylon) saying, 4 Thus saith the Lord of hosts, the God of Israel, unto all that are carried away captives, whom I have caused to be carried away from Jerusalem unto Babylon; 5 Build ye houses, and dwell in them; and plant gardens, and eat the fruit of them; 6 Take ye wives, and beget sons and daughters; and take wives for your sons, and give your daughters to husbands, that they may bear sons and daughters; that ye may be increased there, and not diminished. 7 And seek the peace of the city whither I have caused you to be carried away captives, and pray unto the Lord for it: for in the peace thereof shall ye have peace. 8 For thus saith the Lord of hosts, the God of Israel; Let not your

prophets and your diviners, that be in the midst of you, deceive you, neither hearken to your dreams which ye cause to be dreamed. 9 For they prophesy falsely unto you in my name: I have not sent them, saith the Lord. 10 For thus saith the Lord, That after seventy years be accomplished at Babylon I will visit you, and perform my good word toward you, in causing you to return to this place. 11 For I know the thoughts that I think toward you, saith the Lord, thoughts of peace, and not of evil, to give you an expected end. 12 Then shall ye call upon me, and ye shall go and pray unto me, and I will hearken unto you. 13 And ye shall seek me, and find me, when ye shall search for me with all your heart. 14 And I will be found of you, saith the Lord: and I will turn away your captivity, and I will gather you from all the nations, and from all the places whither I have driven you, saith the Lord; and I will bring you again into the place whence I caused you to be carried away captive.

29.1-14 The letter. Jeremiah is the amanuensis, but this letter is from God. This letter is an instruction manual of sorts on how to survive in Babylon. The captives are instructed to build houses, get married and have families, and seek the peace of the city. They are going to be there 70 years so God is instructing them how to survive and prosper. The people are encouraged to plant gardens, and enjoy the fruit of their husbandry. They are warned to not allow the false prophets to deceive them. When the 70 years has run it's course they will return to the land. God emphatically tells them His thoughts toward them are of peace and not evil (bad or sad). They will seek God and find Him when they seek Him with their whole heart. That will signal the beginning of the turning of the captivity. That concept of the people of God seeking Him with the whole heart is the secret to all spiritual success and healing. It would be the catalyst to bring them out of Babylon and repatriate the Promised Land.

29.15-23 Because ye have said, The Lord hath raised us up prophets in Babylon; 16 Know that thus saith the Lord of the king that sitteth upon the throne of David, and of all the people that dwelleth in this city, and of your brethren that are not gone forth with you into captivity; 17 Thus saith the Lord of hosts; Behold, I will send upon them the sword, the famine, and the pestilence, and will make them like vile figs, that cannot be eaten, they are so evil. 18 And I will persecute them with the sword, with the famine, and with the pestilence, and will deliver them to be removed to all the kingdoms of the earth, to be a curse, and an astonishment, and an hissing, and a reproach, among all the nations whither I have driven them: 19 Because they have not hearkened to my words, saith the Lord, which I sent unto them by my servants the prophets, rising up early and sending them; but ye would not hear, saith the Lord. 20 Hear ye therefore the word of the Lord, all ye of the captivity, whom I have sent from Jerusalem to Babylon: 21 Thus saith the Lord of hosts, the God of Israel, of Ahab the son of Kolaiah, and of Zedekiah the son of Maaseiah, which prophesy a lie unto you in my name; Behold, I will deliver them into the hand of Nebuchadrezzar king of Babylon; and he shall slay them before your eyes; 22 And of them shall be taken up a curse by all the captivity of Judah which are in Babylon, saying, The Lord make thee like Zedekiah and like Ahab, whom the king of Babylon roasted in the fire; 23 Because they have committed villany in Israel, and have committed adultery with their neighbours' wives, and have spoken lying words in my name, which I have not commanded them; even I know, and am a witness, saith the Lord.

29.15-23 Ahab and Zedekiah. The recurring problem of false prophets arises again. We are not privy to know anything about these two pseudo-prophets. They are named and their sins are listed. They commit adultery with their neighbor's wives and they commit folly in Israel. The term "commit folly" is used of gross sins of uncleanness (Gen 34.7). The text infers they were guilty of some crime against the state and therefore suffered the fate of the Babylonian justice system, being roasted by fire. These prophets the people thought had been raised up in Babylon were revealed by God for what they were. They were charlatans.

29.24-32 Thus shalt thou also speak to Shemaiah the Nehelamite, saying, 25 Thus speaketh the Lord of hosts, the God of Israel, saying, Because thou hast sent letters in thy name unto all the people that are at Jerusalem, and to Zephaniah the son of Maaseiah the priest, and to all the priests, saying, 26 The Lord hath made thee priest in the stead of Jehoiada the priest, that ye should be officers in the house of the Lord, for every man that is mad, and maketh himself a prophet, that thou shouldest put him in prison, and in the stocks. 27 Now therefore why hast thou not reproved Jeremiah of Anathoth, which maketh himself a prophet to you? 28 For therefore he sent unto us in Babylon, saying, This captivity is long: build ye houses, and dwell in them; and plant gardens, and eat the fruit of them. 29 And Zephaniah the priest read this letter in the ears of Jeremiah the prophet. 30 Then came the word of the Lord unto Jeremiah, saying, 31 Send to all them of the captivity, saying, Thus saith the Lord concerning Shemaiah the Nehelamite; Because that Shemaiah hath prophesied unto you, and I sent him not, and he caused you to trust in a lie: 32 Therefore thus saith the Lord; Behold, I will punish Shemaiah

the Nehelamite, and his seed: he shall not have a man to dwell among this people; neither shall he behold the good that I will do for my people, saith the Lord; because he hath taught rebellion against the Lord.

29.24-32 Shemaiah's false prophecy. The letter Jeremiah wrote to the exiles had kindled the indignation of the false prophets in Babylon. These prophets were predicting speedy return from Babylon. One of these false prophets wrote a letter back to Zephaniah who was the highest-ranking priest. Shemaiah had hopes that Zephaniah would chastise Jeremiah. Zephaniah reads the letter to Jeremiah and God speaks judgment against Shemaiah. Shemaiah is told his race should perish and not survive when the repatriation happens. His false dreams and utterances doomed any future generations from his lineage.

Chapter 30

30.1-17 The word that came to Jeremiah from the Lord, saying, 2 Thus speaketh the Lord God of Israel, saying, Write thee all the words that I have spoken unto thee in a book. 3 For, lo, the days come, saith the Lord, that I will bring again the captivity of my people Israel and Judah, saith the Lord: and I will cause them to return to the land that I gave to their fathers, and they shall possess it. 4 And these are the words that the Lord spake concerning Israel and concerning Judah. 5 For thus saith the Lord; We have heard a voice of trembling, of fear, and not of peace. 6 Ask ye now, and see whether a man doth travail with child? wherefore do I see every man with his hands on his loins, as a woman in travail, and all faces are turned into paleness? 7 Alas! for that day is great, so that none is like it: it is even the time of Jacob's trouble, but he shall be saved out of it. 8 For it shall come to pass in that day, saith the Lord of hosts, that I will break his yoke from off thy neck, and will burst thy bonds, and strangers shall no more serve themselves of him: 9 But they shall serve the Lord their God, and David their king, whom I will raise up unto them. 10 Therefore fear thou not, O my servant Jacob, saith the Lord; neither be dismayed, O Israel: for, lo, I will save thee from afar, and thy seed from the land of their captivity; and Jacob shall return, and shall be in rest, and be quiet, and none shall make him afraid. 11 For I am with thee, saith the Lord, to save thee: though I make a full end of all nations whither I have scattered thee, yet I will not make a full end of thee: but I will correct thee in measure, and will not leave thee altogether unpunished. 12 For thus saith the Lord, Thy bruise is incurable, and thy wound is grievous. 13 There is none to plead thy cause, that thou mayest be bound up: thou hast no healing medicines. 14 All thy lovers have forgotten thee; they seek thee not; for I have wounded thee with the wound of an enemy, with the chastisement of a cruel one, for the multitude of thine iniquity; because thy sins were increased. 15 Why criest thou for thine affliction? thy sorrow is incurable for the multitude of thine iniquity: because thy sins were increased, I have done these things unto thee. 16 Therefore all they that devour thee shall be devoured; and all thine adversaries, every one of them, shall go into captivity; and they that spoil thee shall be a spoil, and all that prey upon thee will I give for a prey. 17 For I will restore health unto thee, and I will heal thee of thy wounds, saith the Lord; because they called thee an Outcast, saying, This is Zion, whom no man seeketh after.

30.1-17 Jacob's trouble. This is a term that will eventually come to encompass the entire time of the dispersion of 70 years and also the worldwide diaspora following the destruction of Jerusalem in 70 AD. This is the lineated list of sins for why God is invoking Jacob's trouble. The captivity will occur, but it will pass when the people are purged from their iniquities. God is correcting his children, for if He does not, they are not truly His children. The lovers Judah had pursued, when they forsook God, are nowhere to be found. God is faithful and never leaves Judah. The axiom "actions speak louder than words" is here on display in graphic color. Who truly loves Judah? God proves His love is constant and true. The yearning of God for His people shows that when no one else wanted them, God was faithful. Jacob's trouble is to refine Israel and make them pure. Jacob's trouble will eventually bring salvation, righteousness, peace, and the coming Messiah. Jacob's trouble is to create Jacob as a treasure in all the earth.

30.18-24 Thus saith the Lord; Behold, I will bring again the captivity of Jacob's tents, and have mercy on his dwellingplaces; and the city shall be builded upon her own heap, and the palace shall remain after the manner thereof. 19 And out of them shall proceed thanksgiving and the voice of them that make merry: and I will multiply them, and they shall not be few; I will also glorify them, and they shall not be small. 20 Their children also shall be as aforetime, and their congregation shall be established before me, and I will punish all that oppress them. 21 And their nobles shall be of themselves, and their governor shall proceed from the midst of them; and I will cause him to draw near, and he shall approach unto me: for who is this that engaged his heart to approach unto me? saith the Lord. 22 And ye shall be my people, and I will be your God. 23 Behold, the whirlwind of the Lord goeth forth with fury, a continuing whirlwind: it shall fall with pain upon the head of the wicked. 24 The fierce anger of the Lord shall not return, until he hath done it, and until he have performed the intents of his heart: in the latter days ye shall consider it.

30.18-24 Hope. God never leaves His people without hope, no matter how hopeless it appears to be. God documents in detail the restoration. In chapters 30-33 God gives messages of consolation to His hurting people. When

God's anger has burned out, they will again be the apple of His eye. The anarthrous countryside of burned, destroyed, cities will be restored and inhabited. Israel shall yet live. Israel is not cast off forever.

Chapter 31

31.1-5 At the same time, saith the Lord, will I be the God of all the families of Israel, and they shall be my people. 2 Thus saith the Lord, The people which were left of the sword found grace in the wilderness; even Israel, when I went to cause him to rest. 3 The Lord hath appeared of old unto me, saying, Yea, I have loved thee with an everlasting love: therefore with lovingkindness have I drawn thee. 4 Again I will build thee, and thou shalt be built, O virgin of Israel: thou shalt again be adorned with thy tabrets, and shalt go forth in the dances of them that make merry. 5 Thou shalt yet plant vines upon the mountains of Samaria: the planters shall plant, and shall eat them as common things.

31.1-5 This chapter introduces the greatest revelation of the Old Testament, the New Covenant. God begins by reaffirming His desire and commitment to the nation He established on Sinai. God's love is everlasting and is accompanied with loving-kindness (which includes both kindness and reproach). The nation of Israel is the personal representative of God's law on planet earth. Israel is not forsaken; she is being purified by the fire of captivity in Babylon. The northern kingdom, which has been gone for over a hundred years, will also be restored.

31.6-11 For there shall be a day, that the watchmen upon the mount Ephraim shall cry, Arise ye, and let us go up to Zion unto the Lord our God. 7 For thus saith the Lord; Sing with gladness for Jacob, and shout among the chief of the nations: publish ye, praise ye, and say, O Lord, save thy people, the remnant of Israel. 8 Behold, I will bring them from the north country, and gather them from the coasts of the earth, and with them the blind and the lame, the woman with child and her that travaileth with child together: a great company shall return thither. 9 They shall come with weeping, and with supplications will I lead them: I will cause them to walk by the rivers of waters in a straight way, wherein they shall not stumble: for I am a father to Israel, and Ephraim is my firstborn. 10 Hear the word of the Lord, O ye nations, and declare it in the isles afar off, and say, He that scattered Israel will gather him, and keep him, as a shepherd doth his flock. 11 For the Lord hath redeemed Jacob, and ransomed him from the hand of him that was stronger than he.

31.6-11 The watchmen. One of the key elements of the restoration is a return to Godly leadership. Judah and Israel had been plagued by false prophets and this must be purged from the nation along with idolatry. This does occur and when the return from Babylon eventuates, God sends faithful voices like Ezra, Nehemiah, and Zechariah. These true men of God keep the nation true to God. The method they use is the written word. Prophets are held to the rule of the Word. This is the principal Jesus taught, and was also adopted by the Apostle Paul. In the New Testament God gives a five-fold ministry to lead the church. This consists of Apostles, Prophets, Evangelists, Pastors and teachers (Eph 4.11). These offices are the watchmen of the New Testament.

31.12-14 Therefore they shall come and sing in the height of Zion, and shall flow together to the goodness of the Lord, for wheat, and for wine, and for oil, and for the young of the flock and of the herd: and their soul shall be as a watered garden; and they shall not sorrow any more at all. 13 Then shall the virgin rejoice in the dance, both young men and old together: for I will turn their mourning into joy, and will comfort them, and make them rejoice from their sorrow. 14 And I will satiate the soul of the priests with fatness, and my people shall be satisfied with my goodness, saith the Lord.

31.12-14 The return. The repatriation will be characterized by singing, bountiful crops, rejoicing, and with satisfied priests.

31.15-17 Thus saith the Lord; A voice was heard in Ramah, lamentation, and bitter weeping; Rahel weeping for her children refused to be comforted for her children, because they were not. 16 Thus saith the Lord; Refrain thy voice from weeping, and thine eyes from tears: for thy work shall be rewarded, saith the Lord; and they shall come again from the land of the enemy. 17 And there is hope in thine end, saith the Lord, that thy children shall come again to their own border.

31.15-17 Rachel weeping. This passage is interesting for it's use in the New Testament. Here it means simply dry your eyes and do not weep for those who died, but rejoice in the restoration. In the New Testament when Herod the King has all the children under two years old murdered, this passage is quoted. In the most basic elemental way this speaks of grief. Ramah was north of Jerusalem in the country of Benjamin and had been the scene of much travail. It had come to represent deep sorrow over what could have been. Therefore the New Testament writer applies it to the death of the innocent recorded in Matt 2.16. In this passage Jeremiah speaks of the weeping as for the slain of Samaria and the coming destruction of Jerusalem.

31.18-20 I have surely heard Ephraim bemoaning himself thus; Thou hast chastised me, and I was chastised, as a bullock unaccustomed to the yoke: turn thou me, and I shall be turned; for thou art the Lord my God. 19 Surely after that I was turned, I repented; and after that I was instructed, I smote upon my thigh: I was ashamed, yea, even confounded, because I did bear the reproach of my youth. 20 Is Ephraim my dear son? is he a pleasant child? for since I spake against him, I do earnestly remember him still: therefore my bowels are troubled for him; I will surely have mercy upon him, saith the Lord.

31.18-20 Ephraim. The poignant picture here is of the ten tribes of the north returning to the Lord. The ten tribes are represented by the term Ephraim. This is the path being shown to Judah to follow as well. The message is vivid; use this approaching dispersion as the doorway to return to God.

31.21-30 Set thee up waymarks, make thee high heaps: set thine heart toward the highway, even the way which thou wentest: turn again, O virgin of Israel, turn again to these thy cities. 22 How long wilt thou go about, O thou backsliding daughter? for the Lord hath created a new thing in the earth, A woman shall compass a man. 23 Thus saith the Lord of hosts, the God of Israel; As yet they shall use this speech in the land of Judah and in the cities thereof, when I shall bring again their captivity; The Lord bless thee, O habitation of justice, and

mountain of holiness. 24 And there shall dwell in Judah itself, and in all the cities thereof together, husbandmen, and they that go forth with flocks. 25 For I have satiated the weary soul, and I have replenished every sorrowful soul. 26 Upon this I awaked, and beheld; and my sleep was sweet unto me. 27 Behold, the days come, saith the Lord, that I will sow the house of Israel and the house of Judah with the seed of man, and with the seed of beast. 28 And it shall come to pass, that like as I have watched over them, to pluck up, and to break down, and to throw down, and to destroy, and to afflict; so will I watch over them, to build, and to plant, saith the Lord. 29 In those days they shall say no more, The fathers have eaten a sour grape, and the children's teeth are set on edge. 30 But every one shall die for his own iniquity: every man that eateth the sour grape, his teeth shall be set on edge.

31.21-30 The promise. God promises He will be as diligent to restore, as He has been to judge. The onus of responsibility is being transferred to every individual, and each person will be judged for their own iniquity. This will be the final judgment of the people of God as a nation. All future judgment will be about individual failure and lack of repentance. This is a major shift in God's economy and introduces the greatest shift of the purpose of God in the Old Testament. This is the tremor before the earthquake.

31.31-40 Behold, the days come, saith the Lord, that I will make a new covenant with the house of Israel, and with the house of Judah: 32 Not according to the covenant that I made with their fathers in the day that I took them by the hand to bring them out of the land of Egypt; which my covenant they brake, although I was an husband unto them, saith the Lord: 33 But this shall be the covenant that I will make with the house of Israel;

After those days, saith the Lord, I will put my law in their inward parts, and write it in their hearts; and will be their God, and they shall be my people. 34 And they shall teach no more every man his neighbour, and every man his brother, saying, Know the Lord: for they shall all know me, from the least of them unto the greatest of them, saith the Lord: for I will forgive their iniquity, and I will remember their sin no more. 35 Thus saith the Lord, which giveth the sun for a light by day, and the ordinances of the moon and of the stars for a light by night, which divideth the sea when the waves thereof roar; The Lord of hosts is his name: 36 If those ordinances depart from before me, saith the Lord, then the seed of Israel also shall cease from being a nation before me for ever. 37 Thus saith the Lord; If heaven above can be measured, and the foundations of the earth searched out beneath, I will also cast off all the seed of Israel for all that they have done, saith the Lord. 38 Behold, the days come, saith the Lord, that the city shall be built to the Lord from the tower of Hananeel unto the gate of the corner. 39 And the measuring line shall yet go forth over against it upon the hill Gareb, and shall compass about to Goath. 40 And the whole valley of the dead bodies, and of the ashes, and all the fields unto the brook of Kidron, unto the corner of the horse gate toward the east, shall be holy unto the Lord; it shall not be plucked up, nor thrown down any more for ever.

31.31-40 The new covenant. This is the earthquake that shakes the foundation of everything God had revealed for over 1300 years. The pride of Israel was their calling and was based on Abraham being called in 1921 BC. The nation became the personal property of God on Sinai with the giving of the law. That law was collective and was therefore judged collectively. Now the seismic shift is announced. Those days are going to pass and a new day is dawning. Each individual will be responsible for the law in his own heart. This is the moment the entire plan of God shifts. It includes a New Covenant. This will be the culmination of all God's covenants with His people and will expand His people to include gentile nations. The covenant written on tables of stone will now be written on the human heart. This seismic shift entails the revelation of new concepts that Jesus brought when He came to earth. Jesus did not abolish the law, He fulfilled the law. Many of the concepts of the Old Covenant were introduced in new terms. Adultery was now in looking at a woman with lust because it was a matter of the heart (Matt 5.28). Jeremiah had been laying the groundwork for the heart as the center of God's plan in message after message, and now he reveals the complete portrait of God's plan. This plan shifts in epic proportions the relationship of people from a national relationship to a personal relationship. This would be introduced in Acts 2.1-4 with the outpouring of the Holy Ghost. God would come to live in the heart of individual believers. Paul expounds on this by acknowledging the individual is actually the temple of God and God dwells inside the believer. This New Testament revelation was launched here by Jeremiah and is the foundation of the New Covenant. The great discussion of whether the church replaces Israel in God's everlasting plan is simplified here to reveal God's plan is simply expanded to include gentiles. This is explained in many New Testament passages, and also in other passages of the Major Prophets (Is 49.22). The message is no longer national, it is personal. All believers will now be called "my people" by God (2 Cor 6.16, Gal 3.26-29). This is the seismic shift. This is advanced further in the New Testament when the Gentiles are brought into the church in Acts 10. The council of the Apostles endorses this in the conference in Acts 15. The ensuing missionary journeys of Paul cement this seismic shift forever. The Gospel was now a personal responsibility and engulfed the whole world. Paul the Apostle speaks of this as common knowledge when he refers to the churches of Galatia as the Israel of God (Gal 6.16).

Chapter 32

32.1-15 The word that came to Jeremiah from the Lord in the tenth year of Zedekiah king of Judah, which was the eighteenth year of Nebuchadrezzar. 2 For then the king of Babylon's army besieged Jerusalem: and Jeremiah the prophet was shut up in the court of the prison, which was in the king of Judah's house. 3 For Zedekiah king of Judah had shut him up, saying, Wherefore dost thou prophesy, and say, Thus saith the Lord, Behold, I will give this city into the hand of the king of Babylon, and he shall take it; 4 And Zedekiah king of Judah shall not escape out of the hand of the Chaldeans, but shall surely be delivered into the hand of the king of Babylon, and shall speak with him mouth to mouth, and his eyes shall behold his eyes; 5 And he shall lead Zedekiah to Babylon, and there shall he be until I visit him, saith the Lord: though ye fight with the Chaldeans, ye shall not prosper. 6 And Jeremiah said, The word of the Lord came unto me, saying, 7 Behold, Hanameel the son of Shallum thine uncle shall come unto thee saying, Buy thee my field that is in Anathoth: for the right of redemption is thine to buy it. 8 So Hanameel mine uncle's son came to me in the court of the prison according to the word of the Lord, and said unto me, Buy my field, I pray thee, that is in Anathoth, which is in the country of

Benjamin: for the right of inheritance is thine, and the redemption is thine; buy it for thyself. Then I knew that this was the word of the Lord. 9 And I bought the field of Hanameel my uncle's son, that was in Anathoth, and weighed him the money, even seventeen shekels of silver. 10 And I subscribed the evidence, and sealed it, and took witnesses, and weighed him the money in the balances. 11 So I took the evidence of the purchase, both that which was sealed according to the law and custom, and that which was open: 12 And I gave the evidence of the purchase unto Baruch the son of Neriah, the son of Maaseiah, in the sight of Hanameel mine uncle's son, and in the presence of the witnesses that subscribed the book of the purchase, before all the Jews that sat in the court of the prison. 13 And I charged Baruch before them, saying, 14 Thus saith the Lord of hosts, the God of Israel; Take these evidences, this evidence of the purchase, both which is sealed, and this evidence which is open; and put them in an earthen vessel, that they may continue many days. 15 For thus saith the Lord of hosts, the God of Israel; Houses and fields and vineyards shall be possessed again in this land.

32.1-15 The purchase. The setting of this chapter is amazing. Jeremiah has been locked up in jail by the King for his unpopular prophecies. God speaks to Jeremiah in the jail and tells him his uncle would be coming to see him. Jeremiah's uncle would offer to sell a parcel of land in Anathoth, which is the hometown of Jeremiah. Jeremiah buys the field for 17 shekels of silver. This is yet another living message from God to the nation. God will bring them back to their homeland; so don't sell your inheritance.

32.16-44 Now when I had delivered the evidence of the purchase unto Baruch the son of Neriah, I prayed unto

the Lord, saying, 17 Ah Lord God! behold, thou hast made the heaven and the earth by thy great power and stretched out arm, and there is nothing too hard for thee: 18 Thou shewest lovingkindness unto thousands, and recompensest the iniquity of the fathers into the bosom of their children after them: the Great, the Mighty God, the Lord of hosts, is his name, 19 Great in counsel, and mighty in work: for thine eyes are open upon all the ways of the sons of men: to give every one according to his ways, and according to the fruit of his doings: 20 Which hast set signs and wonders in the land of Egypt, even unto this day, and in Israel, and among other men; and hast made thee a name, as at this day; 21 And hast brought forth thy people Israel out of the land of Egypt with signs, and with wonders, and with a strong hand, and with a stretched out arm, and with great terror; 22 And hast given them this land, which thou didst swear to their fathers to give them, a land flowing with milk and honey; 23 And they came in, and possessed it; but they obeyed not thy voice, neither walked in thy law; they have done nothing of all that thou commandedst them to do: therefore thou hast caused all this evil to come upon them: 24 Behold the mounts, they are come unto the city to take it; and the city is given into the hand of the Chaldeans, that fight against it, because of the sword, and of the famine, and of the pestilence: and what thou hast spoken is come to pass; and, behold, thou seest it. 25 And thou hast said unto me, O Lord God, Buy thee the field for money, and take witnesses; for the city is given into the hand of the Chaldeans. 26 Then came the word of the Lord unto Jeremiah, saying, 27 Behold, I am the Lord, the God of all flesh: is there any thing too hard for me? 28 Therefore thus saith the Lord; Behold, I will give this city into the hand of the Chaldeans, and into the hand of Nebuchadrezzar king of Babylon, and he shall take it: 29 And the Chaldeans, that fight against this city, shall come and set fire on this city, and burn it with the houses, upon whose roofs they have offered incense unto Baal, and poured out drink offerings unto other gods, to provoke me to anger. 30 For the children of Israel and the children of Judah have only done evil before me from their youth: for the children of Israel have only provoked me to anger with the work of their hands, saith the Lord. 31 For this city hath been to me as a provocation of mine anger and of my fury from the day that they built it even unto this day; that I should remove it from before my face, 32 Because of all the evil of the children of Israel and of the children of Judah, which they have done to provoke me to anger, they, their kings, their princes, their priests, and their prophets, and the men of Judah, and the inhabitants of Jerusalem. 33 And they have turned unto me the back, and not the face: though I taught them, rising up early and teaching them, yet they have not hearkened to receive instruction. 34 But they set their abominations in the house, which is called by my name, to defile it. 35 And they built the high places of Baal, which are in the valley of the son of Hinnom, to cause their sons and their daughters to pass through the fire unto Molech; which I commanded them not, neither came it into my mind, that they should do this abomination, to cause Judah to sin. 36 And now therefore thus saith the Lord, the God of Israel, concerning this city, whereof ye say, It shall be delivered into the hand of the king of Babylon by the sword, and by the famine, and by the pestilence; 37 Behold, I will gather them out of all countries, whither I have driven them in mine anger, and in my fury, and in great wrath; and I will bring them again unto this place, and I will cause them to dwell safely: 38 And they shall be my people, and I will be their God: 39 And I will give them one heart, and one way, that they may fear me for ever, for the good of them, and of their children after them: **40 And I will make an everlasting covenant with them, that I will not turn away from them, to do them good; but I will put my fear in their hearts, that they shall not depart from me. 41 Yea, I will rejoice over them to do them good, and I will plant them in this land assuredly with my whole heart and with my whole soul. 42 For thus saith the Lord; Like as I have brought all this great evil upon this people, so will I bring upon them all the good that I have promised them. 43 And fields shall be bought in this land, whereof ye say, It is desolate without man or beast; it is given into the hand of the Chaldeans. 44 Men shall buy fields for money, and subscribe evidences, and seal them, and take witnesses in the land of Benjamin, and in the places about Jerusalem, and in the cities of Judah, and in the cities of the mountains, and in the cities of the valley, and in the cities of the south: for I will cause their captivity to return, saith the Lord.**

32.16-44 The purchase by Jeremiah is tendered in full legal form and witnessed by the proper authorities. Then there is the prayer of the prophet to explain how this purchase is reconciled with the coming of the Chaldeans and the fall of Jerusalem (16-25). God replies He is giving up Jerusalem because of the sins of the people (26-35), but concludes the chapter with the assurance He will gather His people out of all the lands where they have been scattered and make an everlasting covenant with them. The people will again eventually dwell safe and secure and happy in their ancestral home. Jeremiah illustrates this by buying land and sealing the purchase for the future. Jeremiah is again a living sermon. He is the clay on the potter's wheel to be made into whatever vessel the master potter chooses.

Chapter 33

33.1-13 Moreover the word of the Lord came unto Jeremiah the second time, while he was yet shut up in the court of the prison, saying, 2 Thus saith the Lord the maker thereof, the Lord that formed it, to establish it; the Lord is his name; 3 Call unto me, and I will answer thee, and show thee great and mighty things, which thou knowest not. 4 For thus saith the Lord, the God of Israel, concerning the houses of this city, and concerning the houses of the kings of Judah, which are thrown down by the mounts, and by the sword; 5 They come to fight with the Chaldeans, but it is to fill them with the dead bodies of men, whom I have slain in mine anger and in my fury, and for all whose wickedness I have hid my face from this city. 6 Behold, I will bring it health and cure, and I will cure them, and will reveal unto them the abundance of peace and truth. 7 And I will cause the captivity of Judah and the captivity of Israel to return, and will build them, as at the first. 8 And I will cleanse them from all their iniquity, whereby they have sinned against me; and I will pardon all their iniquities, whereby they have sinned, and whereby they have transgressed against me. 9 And it shall be to me a name of joy, a praise and an honour before all the nations of the earth, which shall hear all the good that I do unto them: and they shall fear and tremble for all the goodness and for all the prosperity that I procure unto it. 10 Thus saith the Lord; Again there shall be heard in this place, which ye say shall be desolate without man and without beast, even in the cities of Judah, and in the streets of Jerusalem, that are desolate, without man, and without inhabitant, and without beast, 11 The voice of joy, and the voice of gladness, the voice of the bridegroom, and the voice of the bride, the voice of them that shall say, Praise the Lord of hosts: for the Lord is good; for his mercy endureth for ever: and of them that shall bring the sacrifice of praise into the house of the Lord. For I will cause to return the captivity of the land, as at the first, saith the Lord. 12 Thus saith the Lord of hosts; Again in this place, which is desolate without man and without beast, and in all the cities thereof, shall be an habitation of shepherds causing their flocks to lie down. 13 In the cities of the mountains, in the cities of the vale, and in the cities of the south, and in the land of Benjamin, and in the places about Jerusalem, and in the cities of Judah, shall the flocks pass again under the hands of him that telleth them, saith the Lord.

33.1-13 The prison. Jeremiah is still in the prison when he speaks this prophecy. This is a continuation of Chapter 32. The prophet continues to give details about the coming restoration. He speaks of the destroyed houses and slain men. These issues will be resolved and replaced with health, abundance, and pardon. The people and nation shall be pardoned and cleansed. Joy and praise shall be heard in all the earth. The promise is for the voice of the bride and bridegroom to again be heard. Beasts, ruined cities, and sheepfolds shall all be restored. This attention to great detail is another confirmation of the complete restoration after the complete devastation.

33.14-26 Behold, the days come, saith the Lord, that I will perform that good thing which I have promised unto the house of Israel and to the house of Judah. 15 In those days, and at that time, will I cause the Branch of righteousness to grow up unto David; and he shall execute judgment and righteousness in the land. 16 In those days shall Judah be saved, and Jerusalem shall dwell safely: and this is the name wherewith she shall be called, The Lord our righteousness. 17 For thus saith the Lord; David shall never want a man to sit upon the throne of the house of Israel; 18 Neither shall the priests the Levites want a man before me to offer burnt offerings, and to kindle meat offerings, and to do sacrifice continually. 19 And the word of the Lord came unto Jeremiah, saying, 20 Thus saith the Lord; If ye can break my covenant of the day, and my covenant of the night, and that there should not be day and night in their season; 21 Then may also my covenant be broken with David my servant, that he should not have a son to reign upon his throne; and with the Levites the priests, my ministers. 22 As the host of heaven cannot be numbered, neither the sand of the sea measured: so will I multiply the seed of David my servant, and the Levites that minister unto me. 23 Moreover the word of the Lord came to Jeremiah, saying, 24 Considerest thou not what this people have spoken, saying, The two families which the Lord hath chosen, he hath even cast them off? thus they have despised my people, that they should be no more a nation before them. 25 Thus saith the Lord; If my covenant be not with day and night, and if I have not appointed the ordinances of heaven and earth; 26 Then will I cast away the seed of Jacob and David my servant, so that I will not take any of his seed to be rulers over the seed of Abraham, Isaac, and Jacob: for I will cause their captivity to return, and have mercy on them.

33.14-26 The covenant with David. The shadow of David is still casting it's long influence 400 years after his death. The mark David leaves in the scripture is seen in many places as well as here. The commitment to David by God himself is unparalleled in scripture. We see David with his human quirks and shortcomings. Somewhere deep inside David, God saw something we will never be privy to see. Men have speculated about what that something is for centuries. We may never know the depth and latitude of it completely. It surfaces here again at this critical juncture of Israel's future captivity and restoration. It seems David is never far from God's thoughts. God promises there will always be a descendant of David on the throne. God reaffirms there will be a perpetual priesthood to intervene for man. All of these conditions and promises were fulfilled in the coming of Jesus Christ, the son of David. This is a messianic oracle. Christ is David's son. Christ is our high priest. Christ ever liveth to make intercession for us. God cements this everlasting promise with the challenge; if you can break the covenant of day and night, then you can break the covenant of David. In verse 22 the promise is ascribed to David that was originally given to Abraham. The number of the sand of the sea is used as a metaphor of a number too large to tabulate. The prophecy also includes the number of Levites that minister is also without number. This is fulfilled in the New Testament church where believers are called priests (1 Pet 2.9). They are without number according to Rev 5.10-11. This covenant of David envelopes the covenant of Abraham and expands the covenant to all nations of the world. The prophet Amos saw this with the eye of prophecy when he made reference to the fall of the Northern Kingdom and spoke of the Tabernacle of David (Am 9.11). In Acts chapter 15, at the council of the Apostles discussing the infusion of gentile believers, James recognized the gentiles coming into the church as the moment of the Tabernacle of David (Acts 15.13-16). The two families mentioned in verse 24 have immediate meaning in Israel and Judah, but also secondary meaning in Jew and gentile. The promise has ever been: blessing will be upon all families of the earth (Gen 12.3, 22.18, 26.24, 28.14, Acts 3.25-26, Gal 3.8, Rev 7.9). Jesus Christ, the son of David fulfills every prophetical promise of the Covenant of David.

Chapter 34

34.1-5 The word which came unto Jeremiah from the Lord, when Nebuchadnezzar king of Babylon, and all his army, and all the kingdoms of the earth of his dominion, and all the people, fought against Jerusalem, and against all the cities thereof, saying, 2 Thus saith the Lord, the God of Israel; Go and speak to Zedekiah king of Judah, and tell him, Thus saith the Lord; Behold, I will give this city into the hand of the king of Babylon, and he shall burn it with fire: 3 And thou shalt not escape out of his hand, but shalt surely be taken, and delivered into his hand; and thine eyes shall behold the eyes of the king of Babylon, and he shall speak with thee mouth to mouth, and thou shalt go to Babylon. 4 Yet hear the word of the Lord, O Zedekiah king of Judah; Thus saith the Lord of thee, Thou shalt not die by the sword: 5 But thou shalt die in peace: and with the burnings of thy fathers, the former kings which were before thee, so shall they burn odours for thee; and they will lament thee, saying, Ah lord! for I have pronounced the word, saith the Lord.

34.1-5 Zedekiah. One of the sure signs of a true prophet is to speak future things with absolute accuracy. Here God endorses Jeremiah by this process. The armies of Babylon are encamped against Jerusalem and the fear is palpable.

Jeremiah is instructed to tell the King he will be carried to captivity but will eventually die in peace.

34.6-22 Then Jeremiah the prophet spake all these words unto Zedekiah king of Judah in Jerusalem, 7 When the king of Babylon's army fought against Jerusalem, and against all the cities of Judah that were left, against Lachish, and against Azekah: for these defenced cities remained of the cities of Judah. 8 This is the word that came unto Jeremiah from the Lord, after that the king Zedekiah had made a covenant with all the people which were at Jerusalem, to proclaim liberty unto them; 9 That every man should let his manservant, and every man his maidservant, being an Hebrew or an Hebrewess, go free; that none should serve himself of them, to wit, of a Jew his brother. 10 Now when all the princes, and all the people, which had entered into the covenant, heard that every one should let his manservant, and every one his maidservant, go free, that none should serve themselves of them any more, then they obeyed, and let them go. 11 But afterward they turned, and caused the servants and the handmaids, whom they had let go free, to return, and brought them into subjection for servants and for handmaids. 12 Therefore the word of the Lord came to Jeremiah from the Lord, saying, 13 Thus saith the Lord, the God of Israel; I made a covenant with your fathers in the day that I brought them forth out of the land of Egypt, out of the house of bondmen, saying, 14 At the end of seven years let ye go every man his brother an Hebrew, which hath been sold unto thee; and when he hath served thee six years, thou shalt let him go free from thee: but your fathers hearkened not unto me, neither inclined their ear. 15 And ye were now turned, and had done right in my sight, in proclaiming liberty every man to his neighbour; and ye had made a covenant before me in the house which is called by my name: 16 But ye turned and polluted my name, and caused every man his servant, and every man his handmaid, whom he had set at liberty at their pleasure, to return, and brought them into subjection, to be unto you for servants and for handmaids. 17 Therefore thus saith the Lord; Ye have not hearkened unto me, in proclaiming liberty, every one to his brother, and every man to his neighbour: behold, I proclaim a liberty for you, saith the Lord, to the sword, to the pestilence, and to the famine; and I will make you to be removed into all the kingdoms of the earth. 18 And I will give the men that have transgressed my covenant, which have not performed the words of the covenant which they had made before me, when they cut the calf in twain, and passed between the parts thereof, 19 The princes of Judah, and the princes of Jerusalem, the eunuchs, and the priests, and all the people of the land, which passed between the parts of the calf; 20 I will even give them into the hand of their enemies, and into the hand of them that seek their life: and their dead bodies shall be for meat unto the fowls of the heaven, and to the beasts of the earth. 21 And Zedekiah king of Judah and his princes will I give into the hand of their enemies, and into the hand of them that seek their life, and into the hand of the king of Babylon's army, which are gone up from you. 22 Behold, I will command, saith the Lord, and cause them to return to this city; and they shall fight against it, and take it, and burn it with fire: and I will make the cities of Judah a desolation without an inhabitant.

34.6-22 The emancipation. This interesting note on the actions of the King reflect the unstableness of the nation. First they free all the slaves, then reverse the action and indenture them again. This was initially obedience to the law that required slaves to be freed after six years (Dt 15.12). The people then show their disdain for the law by discarding the word of the Lord. The law of liberty is then applied in reverse by God. With divine sarcasm God proclaims a liberty for them. It is a liberty to the sword, the pestilence, and the famine. It is serious business with God when men make a covenant with God and then forsake the covenant. To those who withdrew liberty from their brother, God withdrew liberty from these same covenant breakers. This concept will become a brick in the foundation of the New Covenant. Jesus proclaimed in the Sermon on the Mount in Matthew of chapters 5 through 7, that with whatsoever judgment we judge, we shall be judged. As with so many concepts of the Old Covenant, Jesus expands the concept of the law of liberty under the New Covenant.

Chapter 35

35.1-19 The word which came unto Jeremiah from the Lord in the days of Jehoiakim the son of Josiah king of Judah, saying, 2 Go unto the house of the Rechabites, and speak unto them, and bring them into the house of the Lord, into one of the chambers, and give them wine to drink. 3 Then I took Jaazaniah the son of Jeremiah, the son of Habaziniah, and his brethren, and all his sons, and the whole house of the Rechabites; 4 And I brought them into the house of the Lord, into the chamber of the sons of Hanan, the son of Igdaliah, a man of God, which was by the chamber of the princes, which was above the chamber of Maaseiah the son of Shallum, the keeper of the door: 5 And I set before the sons of the house of the Rechabites pots full of wine, and cups, and I said unto them, Drink ye wine. 6 But they said, We will drink no wine: for Jonadab the son of Rechab our father commanded us, saying, Ye shall drink no wine, neither ye, nor your sons for ever: 7 Neither shall ye build house, nor sow seed, nor plant vineyard, nor have any: but all your days ye shall dwell in tents; that ye may live many days in the land where ye be strangers. 8 Thus have we obeyed the voice of Jonadab the son of Rechab our father in all that he hath charged us, to drink no wine all our days, we, our wives, our sons, nor our daughters; 9

Nor to build houses for us to dwell in: neither have we vineyard, nor field, nor seed: 10 But we have dwelt in tents, and have obeyed, and done according to all that Jonadab our father commanded us. 11 But it came to pass, when Nebuchadrezzar king of Babylon came up into the land, that we said, Come, and let us go to Jerusalem for fear of the army of the Chaldeans, and for fear of the army of the Syrians: so we dwell at Jerusalem. 12 Then came the word of the Lord unto Jeremiah, saying, 13 Thus saith the Lord of hosts, the God of Israel; Go and tell the men of Judah and the inhabitants of Jerusalem, Will ye not receive instruction to hearken to my words? saith the Lord. 14 The words of Jonadab the son of Rechab, that he commanded his sons not to drink wine, are performed; for unto this day they drink none, but obey their father's commandment: notwithstanding I have spoken unto you, rising early and speaking; but ye hearkened not unto me. 15 I have sent also unto you all my servants the prophets, rising up early and sending them, saying, Return ye now every man from his evil way, and amend your doings, and go not after other gods to serve them, and ye shall dwell in the land which I have given to you and to your fathers: but ye have not inclined your ear, nor hearkened unto me. 16 Because the sons of Jonadab the son of Rechab have performed the commandment of their father, which he commanded them; but this people hath not hearkened unto me: 17 Therefore thus saith the Lord God of hosts, the God of Israel; Behold, I will bring upon Judah and upon all the inhabitants of Jerusalem all the evil that I have pronounced against them: because I have spoken unto them, but they have not heard; and I have called unto them, but they have not answered. 18 And Jeremiah said unto the house of the Rechabites, Thus saith the Lord of hosts, the God of Israel; Because ye have obeyed the commandment of Jonadab your father,

and kept all his precepts, and done according unto all that he hath commanded you: 19 Therefore thus saith the Lord of hosts, the God of Israel; Jonadab the son of Rechab shall not want a man to stand before me for ever.

35.1-19 The Rechabites. This is also one of Jeremiah's most well known messages. The ancestor of the Rechabites, Jonadab, had been a supporter of Jehu when Jehu obliterated the Baal worshippers some hundred plus years before (2K 10.15-16). Jonadab had commanded his descendants to abstain from wine, and live in tents as nomads. This family was still obeying the voice of a dead forefather. By the command of God, Jeremiah brings the family of the Rechabites (who had fled for refuge to Jerusalem before the approach of the Chaldeans) into the chamber of Hanan, the son of Igdaliah in the temple, and sets before them some wine to drink (Jer 35:1-5). This chamber in the temple had been used by Huldah the prophetess and was named after her son Maaseiah. The Rechabites decline to drink, because the head of their family Jonadab, had forbidden them the use of wine, as well as the possession of houses and the cultivation of the soil, and had commanded them to live in tents (Jer 35:6-11). Jeremiah shows this to the people of Judah. The Rechabites faithfully observe the commands and traditions of their ancestor, while the people of Judah transgress the commands of God (Jer 35:12-16). Jeremiah proclaims calamity shall fall upon Judah, but the house of Rechab, will be rewarded for their faithfulness to their ancestor, and shall continue forever (Jer 35:17-19). This concept will also be carried into the New Testament. The Apostle Paul speaks to the Thessalonians about holding the traditions they have been taught (2 Th 2.15).

Chapter 36

36.1-7 And it came to pass in the fourth year of Jehoiakim the son of Josiah king of Judah, that this word came unto Jeremiah from the Lord, saying, 2 Take thee a roll of a book, and write therein all the words that I have spoken unto thee against Israel, and against Judah, and against all the nations, from the day I spake unto thee, from the days of Josiah, even unto this day. 3 It may be that the house of Judah will hear all the evil which I purpose to do unto them; that they may return every man from his evil way; that I may forgive their iniquity and their sin. 4 Then Jeremiah called Baruch the son of Neriah: and Baruch wrote from the mouth of Jeremiah all the words of the Lord, which he had spoken unto him, upon a roll of a book. 5 And Jeremiah commanded Baruch, saying, I am shut up; I cannot go into the house of the Lord: 6 Therefore go thou, and read in the roll, which thou hast written from my mouth, the words of the Lord in the ears of the people in the Lord's house upon the fasting day: and also thou shalt read them in the ears of all Judah that come out of their cities. 7 It may be they will present their supplication before the Lord, and will return every one from his evil way: for great is the anger and the fury that the Lord hath pronounced against this people.

36.1-7 Jehoiakim burns the scroll. These chapters are written in Chiastic structure. God decides to try and reach this sinful people again. He instructs Jeremiah to call for Baruch and have him write down what Jeremiah would speak. Jeremiah writes all the prophecies he has spoken thus far. Jeremiah was still shut up and could not go read the scroll to the temple. Baruch is to go to the temple and read the scroll. Jeremiah has hope that maybe the people will listen and repent.

36.8-19 And Baruch the son of Neriah did according to all that Jeremiah the prophet commanded him, reading in the book the words of the Lord in the Lord's house. 9 And it came to pass in the fifth year of Jehoiakim the son of Josiah king of Judah, in the ninth month, that they proclaimed a fast before the Lord to all the people in Jerusalem, and to all the people that came from the cities of Judah unto Jerusalem. 10 Then read Baruch in the book the words of Jeremiah in the house of the Lord, in the chamber of Gemariah the son of Shaphan the scribe, in the higher court, at the entry of the new gate of the Lord's house, in the ears of all the people. 11 When Michaiah the son of Gemariah, the son of Shaphan, had heard out of the book all the words of the Lord, 12 Then he went down into the king's house, into the scribe's chamber: and, lo, all the princes sat there, even Elishama the scribe, and Delaiah the son of Shemaiah, and Elnathan the son of Achbor, and Gemariah the son of Shaphan, and Zedekiah the son of Hananiah, and all the princes. 13 Then Michaiah declared unto them all the words that he had heard, when Baruch read the book in the ears of the people. 14 Therefore all the princes sent Jehudi the son of Nethaniah, the son of Shelemiah, the son of Cushi, unto Baruch, saying, Take in thine hand the roll wherein thou hast read in the ears of the people,

and come. So Baruch the son of Neriah took the roll in his hand, and came unto them. 15 And they said unto him, Sit down now, and read it in our ears. So Baruch read it in their ears. 16 Now it came to pass, when they had heard all the words, they were afraid both one and other, and said unto Baruch, We will surely tell the king of all these words. 17 And they asked Baruch, saying, Tell us now, How didst thou write all these words at his mouth? 18 Then Baruch answered them, He pronounced all these words unto me with his mouth, and I wrote them with ink in the book. 19 Then said the princes unto Baruch, Go, hide thee, thou and Jeremiah; and let no man know where ye be.

36.8-19 The timing of the scroll. The Bible dates this writing at a specific time, the fifth year of the king in the ninth month. The people had been called to fast for the Lord to give direction about how to turn away the coming war. Jeremiah spoke and Baruch wrote. Baruch then goes to the house of the Lord and reads the scroll. When the princes hear of it they request an audience with Baruch as well. They question Baruch how this writing came about, and he details how it was written. Upon hearing the contents, these princes advise Baruch that he and Jeremiah had better disappear and hide.

36.20-32 And they went in to the king into the court, but they laid up the roll in the chamber of Elishama the scribe, and told all the words in the ears of the king. 21 So the king sent Jehudi to fetch the roll: and he took it out of Elishama the scribe's chamber. And Jehudi read it in the ears of the king, and in the ears of all the princes which stood beside the king. 22 Now the king sat in the winterhouse in the ninth month: and there was a fire on the hearth burning before him. 23 And it came to pass,

that when Jehudi had read three or four leaves, he cut it with the penknife, and cast it into the fire that was on the hearth, until all the roll was consumed in the fire that was on the hearth. 24 Yet they were not afraid, nor rent their garments, neither the king, nor any of his servants that heard all these words. 25 Nevertheless Elnathan and Delaiah and Gemariah had made intercession to the king that he would not burn the roll: but he would not hear them. 26 But the king commanded Jerahmeel the son of Hammelech, and Seraiah the son of Azriel, and Shelemiah the son of Abdeel, to take Baruch the scribe and Jeremiah the prophet: but the Lord hid them. 27 Then the word of the Lord came to Jeremiah, after that the king had burned the roll, and the words which Baruch wrote at the mouth of Jeremiah, saying, 28 Take thee again another roll, and write in it all the former words that were in the first roll, which Jehoiakim the king of Judah hath burned. 29 And thou shalt say to Jehoiakim king of Judah, Thus saith the Lord; Thou hast burned this roll, saying, Why hast thou written therein, saying, The king of Babylon shall certainly come and destroy this land, and shall cause to cease from thence man and beast? 30 Therefore thus saith the Lord of Jehoiakim king of Judah; He shall have none to sit upon the throne of David: and his dead body shall be cast out in the day to the heat, and in the night to the frost. 31 And I will punish him and his seed and his servants for their iniquity; and I will bring upon them, and upon the inhabitants of Jerusalem, and upon the men of Judah, all the evil that I have pronounced against them; but they hearkened not. 32 Then took Jeremiah another roll, and gave it to Baruch the scribe, the son of Neriah; who wrote therein from the mouth of Jeremiah all the words of the book which Jehoiakim king of Judah had burned in the fire: and there were added besides unto them many like words.

36.20-32 Jehoiakim's response to the word of God. When advised the scroll existed, the King asks for it to be brought and read. The king was in his winter house, warm and cozy before a warm fire when the scroll was read to him. When Jehudi starts to read a few pages, Jehudi begins to cut the pages up and cast it into the flames. These people gathered around the King were specifically unafraid of doing this. No doubt they felt secure by the presence of the King. Two men, Elnathan and Delaiah, try to stop this, but they are ignored. In his anger the King says to find Jeremiah and Baruch and detain them, but the Lord hid them. Jeremiah was instructed by God to write another scroll like the first one that had been burned. Jeremiah then passes sentence upon the King for this heinous, impious act of burning the scroll. Jehoiakim will die and his legacy removed. His body will be left unburied, symbolizing his status of being forsaken. This had already been spoken by Jeremiah in chapter 22.18-19. The consequences also extend to all those who were there at the burning of the scroll. They are punished as well. The message here is eternal. Prophets may be hounded and imprisoned. Kings and charlatans may scorn the Word of God, but the Word of God will not perish, it shall be fulfilled.

Chapter 37

37.1-4 And king Zedekiah the son of Josiah reigned instead of Coniah the son of Jehoiakim, whom Nebuchadrezzar king of Babylon made king in the land of Judah. 2 But neither he, nor his servants, nor the people of the land, did hearken unto the words of the Lord, which he spake by the prophet Jeremiah. 3 And Zedekiah the king sent Jehucal the son of Shelemiah and Zephaniah the son of Maaseiah the priest to the prophet Jeremiah, saying, Pray now unto the Lord our God for us. 4 Now Jeremiah came in and went out among the people: for they had not put him into prison.

37.1-4 King Zedekiah. We are left to wonder why this King would call upon Jeremiah for answers when in fact he did not listen or obey. The only reasonable answer is he was hoping for a different answer from Jeremiah.

37.5-10 Then Pharaoh's army was come forth out of Egypt: and when the Chaldeans that besieged Jerusalem heard tidings of them, they departed from Jerusalem. 6 Then came the word of the Lord unto the prophet Jeremiah saying, 7 Thus saith the Lord, the God of Israel; Thus shall ye say to the king of Judah, that sent you unto me to enquire of me; Behold, Pharaoh's army, which is

come forth to help you, shall return to Egypt into their own land. 8 And the Chaldeans shall come again, and fight against this city, and take it, and burn it with fire. 9 Thus saith the Lord; Deceive not yourselves, saying, The Chaldeans shall surely depart from us: for they shall not depart. 10 For though ye had smitten the whole army of the Chaldeans that fight against you, and there remained but wounded men among them, yet should they rise up every man in his tent, and burn this city with fire.

37.5-10 Jeremiah's answer. Jeremiah informs this King that the army he is trusting in will not bring deliverance, but will in fact return home. The Chaldeans will come. The people were listening to deceivers saying that the Chaldeans would depart like Egypt did. The answer is irrevocable. Even if the Chaldean army had only feeble impotent soldiers still they would rise up and burn this city.

37.11-21 And it came to pass, that when the army of the Chaldeans was broken up from Jerusalem for fear of Pharaoh's army, 12 Then Jeremiah went forth out of Jerusalem to go into the land of Benjamin, to separate himself thence in the midst of the people. 13 And when he was in the gate of Benjamin, a captain of the ward was there, whose name was Irijah, the son of Shelemiah, the son of Hananiah; and he took Jeremiah the prophet, saying, Thou fallest away to the Chaldeans. 14 Then said Jeremiah, It is false; I fall not away to the Chaldeans. But he hearkened not to him: so Irijah took Jeremiah, and brought him to the princes. 15 Wherefore the princes were wroth with Jeremiah, and smote him, and put him in prison in the house of Jonathan the scribe: for they had made that the prison. 16 When Jeremiah was entered into the dungeon, and into the cabins, and Jeremiah had remained there many days; 17 Then Zedekiah the king sent, and took him out: and the king asked him secretly in his house, and said, Is there any word from the Lord? And Jeremiah said, There is: for, said he, thou shalt be delivered into the hand of the king of Babylon. 18 Moreover Jeremiah said unto king Zedekiah, What have I offended against thee, or against thy servants, or against this people, that ye have put me in prison? 19 Where are now your prophets which prophesied unto you, saying, The king of Babylon shall not come against you, nor against this land? 20 Therefore hear now, I pray thee, O my lord the king: let my supplication, I pray thee, be accepted before thee; that thou cause me not to return to the house of Jonathan the scribe, lest I die there. 21 Then Zedekiah the king commanded that they should commit Jeremiah into the court of the prison, and that they should give him daily a piece of bread out of the bakers' street, until all the bread in the city were spent. Thus Jeremiah remained in the court of the prison.

37.11-21 Jeremiah attempts to flee. The Chaldean army breaks up and Jeremiah flees out of Jerusalem to separate himself from the people. He is stopped by Irijah who is a son of the priest and is accused of going over to the Chaldeans. Of course this is mere sophistry. The Chaldeans were not even there now. This accusation will result in Jeremiah being charged with being in collusion with the Chaldeans and being imprisoned. The arrest took place "in the midst of the people." The gate was crowded with other Jews hurrying out of Jerusalem, citizens eager to breathe more freely after being cooped up in the overcrowded city. They were anxious to find out what their farms and homesteads had suffered at the hands of the invaders. The leaders are angry with Jeremiah so they beat him and put him in the prison. After being there many days, Zedekiah takes

Jeremiah out and secretly asks is there a word from the Lord? The answer is yes; you will be carried away captive. Jeremiah appeals his imprisonment. Jeremiah taunts Zedekiah with where are your prophets now? Jeremiah is fighting for his life. If he is returned to the prison Jeremiah feels he will die there. There is a compromise. Jeremiah is remanded to the court prison, which is not as threatening or severe. He is given a daily portion of bread from the king. Why? What is his crime? He is imprisoned for speaking God's word faithfully.

Chapter 38

38.1-6 Then Shephatiah the son of Mattan, and Gedaliah the son of Pashur, and Jucal the son of Shelemiah, and Pashur the son of Malchiah, heard the words that Jeremiah had spoken unto all the people, saying, 2 Thus saith the Lord, He that remaineth in this city shall die by the sword, by the famine, and by the pestilence: but he that goeth forth to the Chaldeans shall live; for he shall have his life for a prey, and shall live. 3 Thus saith the Lord, This city shall surely be given into the hand of the king of Babylon's army, which shall take it. 4 Therefore the princes said unto the king, We beseech thee, let this man be put to death: for thus he weakeneth the hands of the men of war that remain in this city, and the hands of all the people, in speaking such words unto them: for this man seeketh not the welfare of this people, but the hurt. 5 Then Zedekiah the king said, Behold, he is in your hand: for the king is not he that can do any thing against you. 6 Then took they Jeremiah, and cast him into the dungeon of Malchiah the son of Hammelech, that was in the court of the prison: and they let down Jeremiah with cords. And in the dungeon there was no water, but mire: so Jeremiah sunk in the mire.

38.1-6 The cistern. The leaders of the country put Jeremiah in the cistern because they feel he is destroying morale among the people. The number of soldiers appears to have decreased. The number of deserters is up. Famine had begun. These all contributed to the charges against Jeremiah. King Zedekiah gives them executive approval to do as they please. They cast Jeremiah into the cistern where there is mire (mud). Jeremiah sinks into the mud and slime. He is at an extremely low point of his life.

38.7-13 Now when Ebedmelech the Ethiopian, one of the eunuchs which was in the king's house, heard that they had put Jeremiah in the dungeon; the king then sitting in the gate of Benjamin; 8 Ebedmelech went forth out of the king's house, and spake to the king saying, 9 My lord the king, these men have done evil in all that they have done to Jeremiah the prophet, whom they have cast into the dungeon; and he is like to die for hunger in the place where he is: for there is no more bread in the city. 10 Then the king commanded Ebedmelech the Ethiopian, saying, Take from hence thirty men with thee, and take up Jeremiah the prophet out of the dungeon, before he die. 11 So Ebedmelech took the men with him, and went into the house of the king under the treasury, and took thence old cast clouts and old rotten rags, and let them down by cords into the dungeon to Jeremiah. 12 And Ebedmelech the Ethiopian said unto Jeremiah, Put now these old cast clouts and rotten rags under thine armholes under the cords. And Jeremiah did so. 13 So they drew up Jeremiah with cords, and took him up out of the dungeon: and Jeremiah remained in the court of the prison.

38.7-13 The rescue. Ebedmelech, one of the eunuchs of the court appeals for Jeremiah's life. The depth of the improvised oubliette must have been quite deep, for they use ropes to let him down and to pull him out. Jeremiah is starving. Zedekiah to his credit allows Jeremiah to be rescued.

38.14-28 Then Zedekiah the king sent, and took Jeremiah the prophet unto him into the third entry that is in the house of the Lord: and the king said unto Jeremiah, I will ask thee a thing; hide nothing from me. 15 Then Jeremiah said unto Zedekiah, If I declare it unto thee, wilt thou not surely put me to death? and if I give thee counsel, wilt thou not hearken unto me? 16 So Zedekiah the king sware secretly unto Jeremiah, saying, As the Lord liveth, that made us this soul, I will not put thee to death, neither will I give thee into the hand of these men that seek thy life. 17 Then said Jeremiah unto Zedekiah, Thus saith the Lord, the God of hosts, the God of Israel; If thou wilt assuredly go forth unto the king of Babylon's princes, then thy soul shall live, and this city shall not be burned with fire; and thou shalt live, and thine house: 18 But if thou wilt not go forth to the king of Babylon's princes, then shall this city be given into the hand of the Chaldeans, and they shall burn it with fire, and thou shalt not escape out of their hand. 19 And Zedekiah the king said unto Jeremiah, I am afraid of the Jews that are fallen to the Chaldeans, lest they deliver me into their hand, and they mock me. 20 But Jeremiah said, They shall not deliver thee. Obey, I beseech thee, the voice of the Lord, which I speak unto thee: so it shall be well unto thee, and thy soul shall live. 21 But if thou refuse to go forth, this is the word that the Lord hath shewed me: 22 And, behold, all the women that are left in the king of Judah's house shall be brought forth to the king of Babylon's princes, and those women shall say, Thy friends have set thee on, and have prevailed against thee: thy feet are

sunk in the mire, and they are turned away back. 23 So they shall bring out all thy wives and thy children to the Chaldeans: and thou shalt not escape out of their hand, but shalt be taken by the hand of the king of Babylon: and thou shalt cause this city to be burned with fire. 24 Then said Zedekiah unto Jeremiah, Let no man know of these words, and thou shalt not die. 25 But if the princes hear that I have talked with thee, and they come unto thee, and say unto thee, Declare unto us now what thou hast said unto the king, hide it not from us, and we will not put thee to death; also what the king said unto thee: 26 Then thou shalt say unto them, I presented my supplication before the king, that he would not cause me to return to Jonathan's house, to die there. 27 Then came all the princes unto Jeremiah, and asked him: and he told them according to all these words that the king had commanded. So they left off speaking with him; for the matter was not perceived. 28 So Jeremiah abode in the court of the prison until the day that Jerusalem was taken: and he was there when Jerusalem was taken.

38.14-28 Political intrigue. Zedekiah is fighting for his political life and he seeks the advice of Jeremiah. Jeremiah asks for immunity from the consequences of the truth. Zedekiah agrees. Jeremiah tells Zedekiah to give himself up to the invaders if he wants to live. The future of the city is in the hands of Zedekiah. If he surrenders, the city is spared. If he refuses, the city will be decimated. Jeremiah further warns the women of the of the King's house will be spared if he surrenders. Zedekiah swears Jeremiah to silence. Zedekiah reveals a plan to deceive the princes of the land if they inquire what Jeremiah has prophesied. Jeremiah agrees with this chicanery toward the princes. It seems he was not advised of God how to handle this conversation so he spoke as the king had requested.

Their ruse worked and the princes did not perceive what had been prophesied. The sad truth was, Jeremiah was the best friend Jerusalem and it's inhabitants had. Their misanthropy was completely misplaced and unjustified. The high point of this chiasm in chapters 34-38 was the burning of the scroll by Jehoiakim. This was an act tantamount to rejecting God as the Lord of the nation. All that is left is the fall of Jerusalem.

Chapter 39

39.1-5 In the ninth year of Zedekiah king of Judah, in the tenth month, came Nebuchadrezzar king of Babylon and all his army against Jerusalem, and they besieged it. 2 And in the eleventh year of Zedekiah, in the fourth month, the ninth day of the month, the city was broken up. 3 And all the princes of the king of Babylon came in, and sat in the middle gate, even Nergalsharezer, Samgarnebo, Sarsechim, Rabsaris, Nergalsharezer, Rabmag, with all the residue of the princes of the king of Babylon. 4 And it came to pass, that when Zedekiah the king of Judah saw them, and all the men of war, then they fled, and went forth out of the city by night, by the way of the king's garden, by the gate betwixt the two walls: and he went out the way of the plain. 5 But the Chaldeans' army pursued after them, and overtook Zedekiah in the plains of Jericho: and when they had taken him, they brought him up to Nebuchadnezzar king of Babylon to Riblah in the land of Hamath, where he gave judgment upon him.

39.1-5 The fall of Jerusalem. The events here happened after an 18-month siege. When the Babylonians were finally closing in, the princes and the King tried to escape. The Chaldeans overtake them and capture Zedekiah and he is brought to Nebuchadnezzar. This long journey of Jeremiah's prophecy is finally being completed.

39.6-10 Then the king of Babylon slew the sons of Zedekiah in Riblah before his eyes: also the king of Babylon slew all the nobles of Judah. 7 Moreover he put out Zedekiah's eyes, and bound him with chains, to carry him to Babylon. 8 And the Chaldeans burned the king's house, and the houses of the people, with fire, and brake down the walls of Jerusalem. 9 Then Nebuzaradan the captain of the guard carried away captive into Babylon the remnant of the people that remained in the city, and those that fell away, that fell to him, with the rest of the people that remained. 10 But Nebuzaradan the captain of the guard left of the poor of the people, which had nothing, in the land of Judah, and gave them vineyards and fields at the same time.

39.6-10 The slaughter. Zedekiah is forced to watch the annihilation of his family and the nobles of Judah. Then the eyes of Zedekiah are put out. The last sight he saw was the fulfillment of Jeremiah's prophecies. Jeremiah's prophecy, about the destruction of the city, if the king did not surrender, is fulfilled.

39.11-18 Now Nebuchadrezzar king of Babylon gave charge concerning Jeremiah to Nebuzaradan the captain of the guard, saying, 12 Take him, and look well to him, and do him no harm; but do unto him even as he shall say unto thee. 13 So Nebuzaradan the captain of the guard sent, and Nebushasban, Rabsaris, and Nergalsharezer, Rabmag, and all the king of Babylon's princes; 14 Even they sent, and took Jeremiah out of the court of the prison, and committed him unto Gedaliah the son of Ahikam the son of Shaphan, that he should

carry him home: so he dwelt among the people. 15 Now the word of the Lord came unto Jeremiah, while he was shut up in the court of the prison, saying, 16 Go and speak to Ebedmelech the Ethiopian, saying, Thus saith the Lord of hosts, the God of Israel; Behold, I will bring my words upon this city for evil, and not for good; and they shall be accomplished in that day before thee. 17 But I will deliver thee in that day, saith the Lord: and thou shalt not be given into the hand of the men of whom thou art afraid. 18 For I will surely deliver thee, and thou shalt not fall by the sword, but thy life shall be for a prey unto thee: because thou hast put thy trust in me, saith the Lord.

39.11-18 Jeremiah is spared. In an amazing display of affirmation, the king of Babylon treats Jeremiah with great care while destroying the king of Judah. Finally Jeremiah is freed. The entire ordeal has been long and arduous. He is not freed by the people who should have honored him. He is freed by the forces that conquered Judah. Here is again the shadow of the coming of Jesus Christ. The very people who should have accepted Jesus crucified him. Jesus is welcomed and honored by those who are not his people, the Gentiles. For all of eternity the words of Jeremiah are inscribed in the scriptures to show God's faithfulness to a prophet who carried out the will of God. The glaring point in this narrative is the almost emotionless narrative. The prophet who showed such passion on other occasions, here is straight forward and matter of fact. His beloved city had been looted and burned. His opposition had been wiped out. This information is given in an almost ho-hum manner. We are left to wonder, was he empty of feeling? Was he half starved? Was he relieved? These things we do not know. What we do know is he was faithful and that always brings vindication.

Chapter 40

40.1-5 The word that came to Jeremiah from the Lord, after that Nebuzaradan the captain of the guard had let him go from Ramah, when he had taken him being bound in chains among all that were carried away captive of Jerusalem and Judah, which were carried away captive unto Babylon. 2 And the captain of the guard took Jeremiah, and said unto him, The Lord thy God hath pronounced this evil upon this place. 3 Now the Lord hath brought it, and done according as he hath said: because ye have sinned against the Lord, and have not obeyed his voice, therefore this thing is come upon you. 4 And now, behold, I loose thee this day from the chains which were upon thine hand. If it seem good unto thee to come with me into Babylon, come; and I will look well unto thee: but if it seem ill unto thee to come with me into Babylon, forbear: behold, all the land is before thee: whither it seemeth good and convenient for thee to go, thither go. 5 Now while he was not yet gone back, he said, Go back also to Gedaliah the son of Ahikam the son of Shaphan, whom the king of Babylon hath made governor over the cities of Judah, and dwell with him among the people: or go wheresoever it seemeth convenient unto thee to go. So the captain of the guard gave him victuals and a reward, and let him go.

40.1-5 Jeremiah is freed. Jeremiah had been held captive at Ramah, a city in the land of Benjamin, about seven miles from Jerusalem. He is brought in chains with the other captives. The captain of the guard of the Chaldeans set Jeremiah free and gave him the choice to either go to Babylon with the captives or return to dwell in Judah. Jeremiah's time of shackles and chains is finally over. At first glance this appears a kindness and a deference. Possibly it is more. The captain is aware all of Jeremiah's words have been fulfilled. It is possible he is giving Jeremiah the open door to pursue his prophetic work wherever Jeremiah feels he should go. The captain recommends staying with the governor Gedaliah in Judah. Jeremiah follows the advice of the captain.

40.6-10 Then went Jeremiah unto Gedaliah the son of Ahikam to Mizpah; and dwelt with him among the people that were left in the land. 7 Now when all the captains of the forces which were in the fields, even they and their men, heard that the king of Babylon had made Gedaliah the son of Ahikam governor in the land, and had committed unto him men, and women, and children, and of the poor of the land, of them that were not carried away captive to Babylon; 8 Then they came to Gedaliah to Mizpah, even Ishmael the son of Nethaniah, and Johanan and Jonathan the sons of Kareah, and Seraiah the son of Tanhumeth, and the sons of Ephai the Netophathite, and Jezaniah the son of a Maachathite, they and their men. 9 And Gedaliah the son of Ahikam the son of Shaphan sware unto them and to their men, saying, Fear not to serve the Chaldeans: dwell in the land, and serve the king of Babylon, and it shall be well with you. 10 As for me, behold, I will dwell at Mizpah, to serve the Chaldeans, which will come unto us: but ye, gather ye wine, and

summer fruits, and oil, and put them in your vessels, and dwell in your cities that ye have taken.

40.6-10 The final part of Jeremiah's ministry. Jeremiah has had his last interview with. Zedekiah and Jerusalem has fallen. That catastrophe brings another chapter of Jeremiah's life to a close. The dramatis personae have made their final exit and only Jeremiah and Baruch remain. Kings and princes, prophets and priests have all passed to death or captivity. The crowded stage of Judah is now almost vacant and the city is in ruins. Jeremiah goes to Mizpah, palace where Samuel judged and where Saul was crowned King. Gedaliah requires those who seek shelter in his protection to pledge service to Babylon. Gedaliah dismisses the people to their homes to farm their lands.

40.11-16 Likewise when all the Jews that were in Moab, and among the Ammonites, and in Edom, and that were in all the countries, heard that the king of Babylon had left a remnant of Judah, and that he had set over them Gedaliah the son of Ahikam the son of Shaphan; 12 Even all the Jews returned out of all places whither they were driven, and came to the land of Judah, to Gedaliah, unto Mizpah, and gathered wine and summer fruits very much. 13 Moreover Johanan the son of Kareah, and all the captains of the forces that were in the fields, came to Gedaliah to Mizpah, 14 And said unto him, Dost thou certainly know that Baalis the king of the Ammonites hath sent Ishmael the son of Nethaniah to slay thee? But Gedaliah the son of Ahikam believed them not. 15 Then Johanan the son of Kareah spake to Gedaliah in Mizpah secretly saying, Let me go, I pray thee, and I will slay Ishmael the son of Nethaniah, and no man shall know it: wherefore should he slay thee, that all the Jews which are gathered unto thee should be scattered, and the remnant

in Judah perish? 16 But Gedaliah the son of Ahikam said unto Johanan the son of Kareah, Thou shalt not do this thing: for thou speakest falsely of Ishmael.

40.11-16 Jews return. When Jews who had escaped to surrounding lands heard Gedaliah was now the governor, many of them returned to their lands. Gedaliah is warned an assassin has been hired to eliminate him. This note is interesting in that Gedaliah does not believe it is true. The accused man Ishmael was of the royal family. We are left to wonder why Gedaliah did not believe the information was accurate. It would ultimately cost him his life.

Chapter 41

41.1-4 Now it came to pass in the seventh month, that Ishmael the son of Nethaniah the son of Elishama, of the seed royal, and the princes of the king, even ten men with him, came unto Gedaliah the son of Ahikam to Mizpah; and there they did eat bread together in Mizpah. 2 Then arose Ishmael the son of Nethaniah, and the ten men that were with him, and smote Gedaliah the son of Ahikam the son of Shaphan with the sword, and slew him, whom the king of Babylon had made governor over the land. 3 Ishmael also slew all the Jews that were with him, even with Gedaliah, at Mizpah, and the Chaldeans that were found there, and the men of war. 4 And it came to pass the second day after he had slain Gedaliah, and no man knew it,

41.1-4 Gedaliah is murdered. The information spoken to Gedaliah that he disbelieved is proven to be true. Gedaliah was only in his appointed position for two months when he was murdered. He is cast into a pit. This day of infamy was commemorated by the post captivity Jews. They honored the day as a day when the hope of living a separated life in the promised land was reached, even though only for two months. The people were now subjected to a new captivity.

41.5-10 That there came certain from Shechem, from Shiloh, and from Samaria, even fourscore men, having their beards shaven, and their clothes rent, and having cut themselves, with offerings and incense in their hand, to bring them to the house of the Lord. 6 And Ishmael the son of Nethaniah went forth from Mizpah to meet them, weeping all along as he went: and it came to pass, as he met them, he said unto them, Come to Gedaliah the son of Ahikam. 7 And it was so, when they came into the midst of the city, that Ishmael the son of Nethaniah slew them, and cast them into the midst of the pit, he, and the men that were with him. 8 But ten men were found among them that said unto Ishmael, Slay us not: for we have treasures in the field, of wheat, and of barley, and of oil, and of honey. So he forbare, and slew them not among their brethren. 9 Now the pit wherein Ishmael had cast all the dead bodies of the men, whom he had slain because of Gedaliah, was it which Asa the king had made for fear of Baasha king of Israel: and Ishmael the son of Nethaniah filled it with them that were slain. 10 Then Ishmael carried away captive all the residue of the people that were in Mizpah, even the king's daughters, and all the people that remained in Mizpah, whom Nebuzaradan the captain of the guard had committed to Gedaliah the son of Ahikam: and Ishmael the son of Nethaniah carried them away captive, and departed to go over to the Ammonites.

41.5-10 Ishmael the son of Nethaniah. This man was not only an executioner, but also a mass murderer and deceiver. Having hidden his diabolical deed against Gedaliah, he now continues his slaughter of 80 more men and casts them into the same pit. 10 of the men bribe him in exchange for their lives. It is a great sadness that these pilgrims were coming back to their homeland only to be intercepted by a murderer and slaughtered for no apparent reason except to hide his crime from being discovered. Ishmael then takes the remaining people as captive back toward Ammon.

41.11-18 But when Johanan the son of Kareah, and all the captains of the forces that were with him, heard of all the evil that Ishmael the son of Nethaniah had done, 12 Then they took all the men, and went to fight with Ishmael the son of Nethaniah, and found him by the great waters that are in Gibeon. 13 Now it came to pass, that when all the people which were with Ishmael saw Johanan the son of Kareah, and all the captains of the forces that were with him, then they were glad. 14 So all the people that Ishmael had carried away captive from Mizpah cast about and returned, and went unto Johanan the son of Kareah. 15 But Ishmael the son of Nethaniah escaped from Johanan with eight men, and went to the Ammonites. 16 Then took Johanan the son of Kareah, and all the captains of the forces that were with him, all the remnant of the people whom he had recovered from Ishmael the son of Nethaniah, from Mizpah, after that he had slain Gedaliah the son of Ahikam, even mighty men of war, and the women, and the children, and the eunuchs, whom he had brought again from Gibeon: 17 And they departed, and dwelt in the habitation of Chimham, which is by Bethlehem, to go to enter into Egypt, 18 Because of the Chaldeans: for they were afraid of them, because Ishmael the son of Nethaniah had slain Gedaliah the son of Ahikam, whom the king of Babylon made governor in the land.

41.11-18 Johanan pursues. When the remaining leaders found out the grisly news of Ishmael's treason, they pursued Ishmael and overtook him at the waters of Gibeon.

The people who are captives saw Johanan and return to him while Ishmael flees for his life. Johanan sought a safe place beyond the reach of Babylon so he went to Chimham, which was toward Egypt. Egypt was the only country not controlled by Babylon. Chimham was a caravansary in the neighborhood of Bethlehem. The Babylonians would view the events mentioned here as rebellion and would react accordingly, so Johanan does not return to Mizpah.

Chapter 42

42.1-6 Then all the captains of the forces, and Johanan the son of Kareah, and Jezaniah the son of Hoshaiah, and all the people from the least even unto the greatest, came near, 2 And said unto Jeremiah the prophet, Let, we beseech thee, our supplication be accepted before thee, and pray for us unto the Lord thy God, even for all this remnant; (for we are left but a few of many, as thine eyes do behold us:) 3 That the Lord thy God may shew us the way wherein we may walk, and the thing that we may do. 4 Then Jeremiah the prophet said unto them, I have heard you; behold, I will pray unto the Lord your God according to your words; and it shall come to pass, that whatsoever thing the Lord shall answer you, I will declare it unto you; I will keep nothing back from you. 5 Then they said to Jeremiah, The Lord be a true and faithful witness between us, if we do not even according to all things for the which the Lord thy God shall send thee to us. 6 Whether it be good, or whether it be evil, we will obey the voice of the Lord our God, to whom we send thee; that it may be well with us, when we obey the voice of the Lord our God.

42.1-6 The prayer for safety. The people left now turn to Jeremiah for direction from God. Jeremiah pledges to give them the unfiltered word from God. The people pledge to obey the word from God without reservation. After so many years of being the bad guy to the leaders of Judah and then finally being appreciated by the Captain of Babylon and Gedaliah, after only two short months Jeremiah is again in chains of bondage.

42.7-22 And it came to pass after ten days, that the word of the Lord came unto Jeremiah. 8 Then called he Johanan the son of Kareah, and all the captains of the forces which were with him, and all the people from the least even to the greatest, 9 And said unto them, Thus saith the Lord, the God of Israel, unto whom ye sent me to present your supplication before him; 10 If ye will still abide in this land, then will I build you, and not pull you down, and I will plant you, and not pluck you up: for I repent me of the evil that I have done unto you. 11 Be not afraid of the king of Babylon, of whom ye are afraid; be not afraid of him, saith the Lord: for I am with you to save you, and to deliver you from his hand. 12 And I will shew mercies unto you, that he may have mercy upon you, and cause you to return to your own land. 13 But if ye say, We will not dwell in this land, neither obey the voice of the Lord your God, 14 Saying, No; but we will go into the land of Egypt, where we shall see no war, nor hear the sound of the trumpet, nor have hunger of bread; and there will we dwell: 15 And now therefore hear the word of the Lord, ye remnant of Judah; Thus saith the Lord of hosts, the God of Israel; If ye wholly set your faces to enter into Egypt, and go to sojourn there; 16 Then it shall come to pass, that the sword, which ye feared, shall overtake you there in the land of Egypt, and the famine, whereof ye were afraid, shall follow close after you there in Egypt; and there ye shall die. 17 So shall it be with all the men that set their faces to go into Egypt to sojourn there; they shall die by the sword, by the famine, and by the pestilence: and none of them shall remain or escape from the evil that I will bring upon them. 18 For thus saith the Lord of hosts, the God of Israel; As mine anger and my fury hath been poured forth upon the inhabitants of Jerusalem; so shall my fury be poured forth upon you, when ye shall enter into Egypt: and ye shall be an execration, and an astonishment, and a curse, and a reproach; and ye shall see this place no more. 19 The Lord hath said concerning you, O ye remnant of Judah; Go ye not into Egypt: know certainly that I have admonished you this day. 20 For ye dissembled in your hearts, when ye sent me unto the Lord your God, saying, Pray for us unto the Lord our God; and according unto all that the Lord our God shall say, so declare unto us, and we will do it. 21 And now I have this day declared it to you; but ye have not obeyed the voice of the Lord your God, nor any thing for the which he hath sent me unto you. 22 Now therefore know certainly that ye shall die by the sword, by the famine, and by the pestilence, in the place whither ye desire to go and to sojourn.

42.7-22 Ten days. After 10 days Jeremiah delivers the news. Stay out of Egypt. The very people, who swore to obey no matter the directive, now show the same color as the nation has for 330 years. These people follow the example of Abraham, Isaac, Jacob and Jeroboam, who had all sought safety in the shadow of Egypt. They will ignore Jeremiah's words and do as they please. The sword and mayhem they seek to escape will engulf them in Egypt. History is hard pressed to present any people at any juncture that so vacillated and disobeyed. Jeremiah unveils their dishonesty and declares they will reap the harvest of their unbelief and disobedience.

How many people were left we do not know. Four years later the captain of Babylon, Nebuzaradan, carried away 745 Jews (52.30).

Chapter 43

43.1-7 And it came to pass, that when Jeremiah had made an end of speaking unto all the people all the words of the Lord their God, for which the Lord their God had sent him to them, even all these words, 2 Then spake Azariah the son of Hoshaiah, and Johanan the son of Kareah, and all the proud men, saying unto Jeremiah, Thou speakest falsely: the Lord our God hath not sent thee to say, Go not into Egypt to sojourn there: 3 But Baruch the son of Neriah setteth thee on against us, for to deliver us into the hand of the Chaldeans, that they might put us to death, and carry us away captives into Babylon. 4 So Johanan the son of Kareah, and all the captains of the forces, and all the people, obeyed not the voice of the Lord, to dwell in the land of Judah. 5 But Johanan the son of Kareah, and all the captains of the forces, took all the remnant of Judah, that were returned from all nations, whither they had been driven, to dwell in the land of Judah; 6 Even men, and women, and children, and the king's daughters, and every person that Nebuzaradan the captain of the guard had left with Gedaliah the son of Ahikam the son of Shaphan, and Jeremiah the prophet, and Baruch the son of Neriah. 7 So they came into the land of Egypt: for they obeyed not the voice of the Lord: thus came they even to Tahpanhes.

43.1-7 Egypt. Once again the leaders revert to form and ignore the words spoken by the prophet Jeremiah. Something as simple as staying put was not obeyed. They show the same stubborn self-will that has destroyed the nation once again, and go to Egypt. They arrive at Tahpanhes, a frontier town in the eastern delta area. Their disobedience is grievous, but their accusation of Jeremiah lying is abominable. They further ascribe the whole intent to Baruch falsely. One thing is very clear; they obeyed not the voice of the Lord.

43.8-13 Then came the word of the Lord unto Jeremiah in Tahpanhes, saying, 9 Take great stones in thine hand, and hide them in the clay in the brickkiln, which is at the entry of Pharaoh's house in Tahpanhes, in the sight of the men of Judah; 10 And say unto them, Thus saith the Lord of hosts, the God of Israel; Behold, I will send and take Nebuchadrezzar the king of Babylon, my servant, and will set his throne upon these stones that I have hid; and he shall spread his royal pavilion over them. 11 And when he cometh, he shall smite the land of Egypt, and deliver such as are for death to death; and such as are for captivity to captivity; and such as are for the sword to the sword. 12 And I will kindle a fire in the houses of the gods of Egypt; and he shall burn them, and carry them away captives: and he shall array himself with the land of Egypt, as a shepherd putteth on his garment; and he shall go forth from thence in peace. 13 He shall break also the images of Bethshemesh, that is in the land of Egypt; and the houses of the gods of the Egyptians shall he burn with fire.

43.8-13 God speaks in Tahpanes. God is not limited geographically, He is omnipresent. God drops the bad news on these disobedient, self-willed, people.

Archaeologists have uncovered a governor's residence at Tahpanes that was used by Pharoah. This is believed to be the area where the stones mentioned here were stacked and Jeremiah informs the people they are not beyond the reach of the Babylonians they were trying to escape. These very stones will be used by Babylon to build upon. God again informs the people they have not escaped the coming judgment. They have gone from the proverbial frying pan into the fire. Their place of refuge will become the pavilion of the King of Babylon. Men never seem to learn you cannot escape from God. The prophecy concludes with the announcement the famous temple of the Sun at Heliopolis would be destroyed. This shows the completeness of Nebuchadnezzar's conquest. This is the city of On mentioned in Gen 41.45, located east of the Nile River and north of Memphis. According to Josephus, Antiquities, 10.9, 7, this occurred in the fifth year after the overthrow of Jerusalem. A text found in the British museum indicates Nebuchadnezzar did invade Egypt in 668-667 BC during the reign of Pharaoh Amasis, Egypt's 26th dynasty. God is not mocked, His word is true.

Chapter 44

44.1-14 The word that came to Jeremiah concerning all the Jews which dwell in the land of Egypt, which dwell at Migdol, and at Tahpanhes, and at Noph, and in the country of Pathros, saying, 2 Thus saith the Lord of hosts, the God of Israel; Ye have seen all the evil that I have brought upon Jerusalem, and upon all the cities of Judah; and, behold, this day they are a desolation, and no man dwelleth therein, 3 Because of their wickedness which they have committed to provoke me to anger, in that they went to burn incense, and to serve other gods, whom they knew not, neither they, ye, nor your fathers. 4 Howbeit I sent unto you all my servants the prophets, rising early and sending them, saying, Oh, do not this abominable thing that I hate. 5 But they hearkened not, nor inclined their ear to turn from their wickedness, to burn no incense unto other gods. 6 Wherefore my fury and mine anger was poured forth, and was kindled in the cities of Judah and in the streets of Jerusalem; and they are wasted and desolate, as at this day. 7 Therefore now thus saith the Lord, the God of hosts, the God of Israel; Wherefore commit ye this great evil against your souls, to cut off from you man and woman, child and suckling, out of Judah, to leave you none to remain; 8 In that ye provoke me unto wrath with the works of your hands, burning incense unto other gods in the land of Egypt, whither ye be gone to dwell, that ye might cut yourselves off, and that ye might be a curse and a reproach among all the nations of the earth? 9 Have ye forgotten the wickedness of your fathers, and the wickedness of the kings of Judah, and the wickedness of their wives, and your own wickedness, and the wickedness of your wives, which they have committed in the land of Judah, and in the streets of Jerusalem? 10 They are not humbled even unto this day, neither have they feared, nor walked in my law, nor in my statutes, that I set before you and before your fathers. 11 Therefore thus saith the Lord of hosts, the God of Israel; Behold, I will set my face against you for evil, and to cut off all Judah. 12 And I will take the remnant of Judah, that have set their faces to go into the land of Egypt to sojourn there, and they shall all be consumed, and fall in the land of Egypt; they shall even be consumed by the sword and by the famine: they shall die, from the least even unto the greatest, by the sword and by the famine: and they shall be an execration, and an astonishment, and a curse, and a reproach. 13 For I will punish them that dwell in the land of Egypt, as I have punished Jerusalem, by the sword, by the famine, and by the pestilence: 14 So that none of the remnant of Judah, which are gone into the land of Egypt to sojourn there, shall escape or remain, that they should return into the land of Judah, to the which they have a desire to return to dwell there: for none shall return but such as shall escape.

44.1-14 God's judgment. Jeremiah now clearly lets the people know they are at the end of their road. There are no more nations to escape to. Their escape to Egypt has only increased God's anger toward them. The farther they ran, the more God's anger increased. He told them to stop; they ran on. The long sordid story of their rebellion goes back for generations and God is tired. None of God's efforts have stemmed the tide of disobedience. He has decided enough is enough and the judgment is forthcoming. Their local does not deter the fire of judgment. It will find them wherever they are and purge their iniquities. The coming punishment in Egypt will mirror the punishment of Jerusalem. None shall escape.

44.15-19 Then all the men which knew that their wives had burned incense unto other gods, and all the women that stood by, a great multitude, even all the people that dwelt in the land of Egypt, in Pathros, answered Jeremiah, saying, 16 As for the word that thou hast spoken unto us in the name of the Lord, we will not hearken unto thee. 17 But we will certainly do whatsoever thing goeth forth out of our own mouth, to burn incense unto the queen of heaven, and to pour out drink offerings unto her, as we have done, we, and our fathers, our kings, and our princes, in the cities of Judah, and in the streets of Jerusalem: for then had we plenty of victuals, and were well, and saw no evil. 18 But since we left off to burn incense to the queen of heaven, and to pour out drink offerings unto her, we have wanted all things, and have been consumed by the sword and by the famine. 19 And when we burned incense to the queen of heaven, and poured out drink offerings unto her, did we make her cakes to worship her, and pour out drink offerings unto her, without our men?

44.15-19 Brazen defiance. The people openly defy Jeremiah and claim they were better off when they worshipped false deities. This is much like the people when they came out of Egypt in the aftermath of the Exodus. They determine to follow the queen of heaven. They are convinced they lost everything because they forsook the queen of heaven.

44.20-30 Then Jeremiah said unto all the people, to the men, and to the women, and to all the people which had given him that answer, saying, 21 The incense that ye burned in the cities of Judah, and in the streets of Jerusalem, ye, and your fathers, your kings, and your princes, and the people of the land, did not the Lord remember them, and came it not into his mind? 22 So that the Lord could no longer bear, because of the evil of your doings, and because of the abominations which ye have committed; therefore is your land a desolation, and an astonishment, and a curse, without an inhabitant, as at this day. 23 Because ye have burned incense, and because ye have sinned against the Lord, and have not obeyed the voice of the Lord, nor walked in his law, nor in his statutes, nor in his testimonies; therefore this evil is happened unto you, as at this day. 24 Moreover Jeremiah said unto all the people, and to all the women, Hear the word of the Lord, all Judah that are in the land of Egypt: 25 Thus saith the Lord of hosts, the God of Israel, saying; Ye and your wives have both spoken with your mouths, and fulfilled with your hand, saying, We will surely perform our vows that we have vowed, to burn incense to the queen of heaven, and to pour out drink offerings unto her: ye will surely accomplish your vows, and surely perform your vows. 26 Therefore hear ye the word of the Lord, all Judah that dwell in the land of Egypt; Behold, I have sworn by my great name, saith the Lord, that my name shall no more be named in the mouth of any man of Judah in all the land of Egypt, saying, The Lord God liveth. 27 Behold, I will watch over them for evil, and not for good: and all the men of Judah that are in the land of Egypt shall be consumed by the sword and by the famine, until there be an end of them. 28 Yet a small number that escape the sword shall return out of the land of Egypt into the land of Judah, and all the remnant of Judah, that are gone into the land of Egypt to sojourn there, shall know whose words shall stand, mine, or their's. 29 And this shall be a sign unto you, saith the Lord, that I will punish you in this place, that ye may know that my words shall surely stand against you for evil: 30 Thus saith the Lord; Behold, I will give Pharaohhophra king of Egypt into the hand of his enemies, and into the hand of them that seek his life; as I gave Zedekiah king of Judah into the hand of Nebuchadrezzar king of Babylon, his enemy, and that sought his life.

44.20-30 Jeremiah's response. The proclivity of man to jettison responsibility is universal. These refugees cannot see themselves as the cause of their dilemma. Their unfaithfulness to God has caused this mayhem and they want to blame others. They have the entire situation inverted as to cause and effect. Jeremiah says to them in effect, as you speak, so shall you have. The most terrible moment in anyone's life is when God steps back and allows people what their own heart desires. As a final sign God gives the Pharoah here, Pharoahhophra, as an example. Most Pharaohs had an additional name and here that name is Hophra, which means broken or lame. Their quest to run from God, return to false deities, ends at the empire of a broken, lame Pharaoh whom Nebuchadnezzar will conquer.

Chapter 45

45.1-5 The word that Jeremiah the prophet spake unto Baruch the son of Neriah, when he had written these words in a book at the mouth of Jeremiah, in the fourth year of Jehoiakim the son of Josiah king of Judah, saying, 2 Thus saith the Lord, the God of Israel, unto thee, O Baruch: 3 Thou didst say, Woe is me now! for the Lord hath added grief to my sorrow; I fainted in my sighing, and I find no rest. 4 Thus shalt thou say unto him, The Lord saith thus; Behold, that which I have built will I break down, and that which I have planted I will pluck up, even this whole land. 5 And seekest thou great things for thyself? seek them not: for, behold, I will bring evil upon all flesh, saith the Lord: but thy life will I give unto thee for a prey in all places whither thou goest.

45.1-5 Baruch. This was Jeremiah's assistant who wrote the scrolls for Jeremiah and read them in the temple (ch 36). This is a personal message to Baruch. Baruch is reproved for his immoderate grief. The land and it's destruction is bigger than his personal discomfort. This is a tendency of people in general. It shows how we can miss the real picture while focused on our personal issues. God was dealing with a big, national problem and Baruch was looking at the narrow view of how it affected him. It is a

Christian discipline to be able to elevate our thoughts and vision to see what God is doing, even if it is through the smoke and haze of personal grief. Jesus and Paul would both endorse and advocate this lifestyle for a Christian (Mt 6.31-34, 1 Ti 6.6-9).

Chapter 46

46.1-12 The word of the Lord which came to Jeremiah the prophet against the Gentiles; 2 Against Egypt, against the army of Pharaohnecho king of Egypt, which was by the river Euphrates in Carchemish, which Nebuchadrezzar king of Babylon smote in the fourth year of Jehoiakim the son of Josiah king of Judah. 3 Order ye the buckler and shield, and draw near to battle. 4 Harness the horses; and get up, ye horsemen, and stand forth with your helmets; furbish the spears, and put on the brigandines. 5 Wherefore have I seen them dismayed and turned away back? and their mighty ones are beaten down, and are fled apace, and look not back: for fear was round about, saith the Lord. 6 Let not the swift flee away, nor the mighty man escape; they shall stumble, and fall toward the north by the river Euphrates. 7 Who is this that cometh up as a flood, whose waters are moved as the rivers? 8 Egypt riseth up like a flood, and his waters are moved like the rivers; and he saith, I will go up, and will cover the earth; I will destroy the city and the inhabitants thereof. 9 Come up, ye horses; and rage, ye chariots; and let the mighty men come forth; the Ethiopians and the Libyans, that handle the shield; and the Lydians, that handle and bend the bow. 10 For this is the day of the Lord God of hosts, a day of vengeance, that he may avenge him of his

adversaries: and the sword shall devour, and it shall be satiate and made drunk with their blood: for the Lord God of hosts hath a sacrifice in the north country by the river Euphrates. 11 Go up into Gilead, and take balm, O virgin, the daughter of Egypt: in vain shalt thou use many medicines; for thou shalt not be cured. 12 The nations have heard of thy shame, and thy cry hath filled the land: for the mighty man hath stumbled against the mighty, and they are fallen both together.

46.1-12 The eye of the prophet turns to foreign nations. There will be seven prophecies in the next chapters (46-51). These prophecies underscore that all nations are under the judicial sentence of God. They were written at various times and are collected here together to present God's judgment on these gentile nations. These prophecies were written earlier in the fourth year of Jehoiakim. Jeremiah speaks to Pharaohnecho the king of Egypt. The king is admonished to prepare his troops. The word from God is that the battle will be intense like a flood. The prophecy is filled with images of horses and chariots and war. The sword is spoken of as being made drunk with blood. The picture of the future of Egypt is dark and foreboding. There is to be no cure, not even in the famed Gilead. As Judah was mortally wounded, so Egypt is also without healing, stumbling to her death. Though the battle is concluded on the plain of Carchemish, it was actually fought in a cosmic realm. This was God fighting Egypt for the shame and cry that had filled the land. The clock of judgment had ticked down to midnight and judgment was loosed on Egypt.

46.13-28 The word that the Lord spake to Jeremiah the prophet, how Nebuchadrezzar king of Babylon should come and smite the land of Egypt. 14 Declare ye in Egypt, and publish in Migdol, and publish in Noph

and in Tahpanhes: say ye, Stand fast, and prepare thee; for the sword shall devour round about thee. 15 Why are thy valiant men swept away? they stood not, because the Lord did drive them. 16 He made many to fall, yea, one fell upon another: and they said, Arise, and let us go again to our own people, and to the land of our nativity, from the oppressing sword. 17 They did cry there, Pharaoh king of Egypt is but a noise; he hath passed the time appointed. 18 As I live, saith the King, whose name is the Lord of hosts, Surely as Tabor is among the mountains, and as Carmel by the sea, so shall he come. 19 O thou daughter dwelling in Egypt, furnish thyself to go into captivity: for Noph shall be waste and desolate without an inhabitant. 20 Egypt is like a very fair heifer, but destruction cometh; it cometh out of the north. 21 Also her hired men are in the midst of her like fatted bullocks; for they also are turned back, and are fled away together: they did not stand, because the day of their calamity was come upon them, and the time of their visitation. 22 The voice thereof shall go like a serpent; for they shall march with an army, and come against her with axes, as hewers of wood. 23 They shall cut down her forest, saith the Lord, though it cannot be searched; because they are more than the grasshoppers, and are innumerable. 24 The daughter of Egypt shall be confounded; she shall be delivered into the hand of the people of the north. 25 The Lord of hosts, the God of Israel, saith; Behold, I will punish the multitude of No, and Pharaoh, and Egypt, with their gods, and their kings; even Pharaoh, and all them that trust in him: 26 And I will deliver them into the hand of those that seek their lives, and into the hand of Nebuchadrezzar king of Babylon, and into the hand of his servants: and afterward it shall be inhabited, as in the days of old, saith the Lord. 27 But fear not thou, O my servant Jacob, and be not dismayed,

O Israel: for, behold, I will save thee from afar off, and thy seed from the land of their captivity; and Jacob shall return, and be in rest and at ease, and none shall make him afraid. 28 Fear thou not, O Jacob my servant, saith the Lord: for I am with thee; for I will make a full end of all the nations whither I have driven thee: but I will not make a full end of thee, but correct thee in measure; yet will I not leave thee wholly unpunished.

46.13-28 The method of Egypt's demise. God chose the king of Babylon to be the tool used to humble mighty Egypt. Jeremiah is to publish the news throughout Egypt, in Migdol, Noph (the royal city), and in Taphanhes (the frontiers). Despite their preparations for war, the valiant men will be swept away. The resistance of the king of Egypt will be nothing more than annoying noise in the path of Nebuchadnezzar. The true King, the Lord of hosts speaks now, as sure as the mountains of Tabor and Carmel are steadfast, so this prophecy is literal. The avenging army of Babylon is coming from the north to reek destruction on Egypt. In the midst of this catastrophe God will protect his chosen people for their future restoration. God's eye is ever on His children wherever they are in the world. Calamity may engulf a nation but God's hand keeps His people safe. Oracles to surrounding nations were also spoken by Amos, Isaiah, and Ezekiel. This chorus of prophetic unison blend into one song of melancholic note. God will bring every work into judgment.

Chapter 47

47.1-7 The word of the Lord that came to Jeremiah the prophet against the Philistines, before that Pharaoh smote Gaza. 2 Thus saith the Lord; Behold, waters rise up out of the north, and shall be an overflowing flood, and shall overflow the land, and all that is therein; the city, and them that dwell therein: then the men shall cry, and all the inhabitants of the land shall howl. 3 At the noise of the stamping of the hoofs of his strong horses, at the rushing of his chariots, and at the rumbling of his wheels, the fathers shall not look back to their children for feebleness of hands; 4 Because of the day that cometh to spoil all the Philistines, and to cut off from Tyrus and Zidon every helper that remaineth: for the Lord will spoil the Philistines, the remnant of the country of Caphtor. 5 Baldness is come upon Gaza; Ashkelon is cut off with the remnant of their valley: how long wilt thou cut thyself? 6 O thou sword of the Lord, how long will it be ere thou be quiet? put up thyself into thy scabbard, rest, and be still. 7 How can it be quiet, seeing the Lord hath given it a charge against Ashkelon, and against the sea shore? there hath he appointed it.

47.1-7 The Philistines. Other prophets also prophesied against the Philistines (Is14.29-31, Ez 25.15-17, Am 1.6-

8 and Zeph 2.4-7). Philistia disappears from the pages of history with the conquests of Nebuchadnezzar. Here Jeremiah foretells their demise and also that of Tyre and Zidon. The Chaldeans are likened to a flood that will overflow this people of Philistia. The population of Philistia are likened to a female who shaves her head, and forsakes her children because the slaughter is so great and terrible. When Jeremiah sees this prophecy he spontaneously cries for the sword of the Lord to be sheathed. God is showing Jeremiah the judgments that will be poured out on the surrounding nations. The Philistines are no more, ever again. They enslaved the Israelites (Joel 3.4-8, 19, Am 1.6-12, Obadiah 10-14), and God removed them forever. The prophetical eye of Jeremiah moves to Moab.

Chapter 48

48.1-12 Against Moab thus saith the Lord of hosts, the God of Israel; Woe unto Nebo! for it is spoiled: Kiriathaim is confounded and taken: Misgab is confounded and dismayed. 2 There shall be no more praise of Moab: in Heshbon they have devised evil against it; come, and let us cut it off from being a nation. Also thou shalt be cut down, O Madmen; the sword shall pursue thee. 3 A voice of crying shall be from Horonaim, spoiling and great destruction. 4 Moab is destroyed; her little ones have caused a cry to be heard. 5 For in the going up of Luhith continual weeping shall go up; for in the going down of Horonaim the enemies have heard a cry of destruction. 6 Flee, save your lives, and be like the heath in the wilderness. 7 For because thou hast trusted in thy works and in thy treasures, thou shalt also be taken: and Chemosh shall go forth into captivity with his priests and his princes together. 8 And the spoiler shall come upon every city, and no city shall escape: the valley also shall perish, and the plain shall be destroyed, as the Lord hath spoken. 9 Give wings unto Moab, that it may flee and get away: for the cities thereof shall be desolate, without any to dwell therein. 10 Cursed be he that doeth the work of the Lord deceitfully, and cursed be he that keepeth back his sword from blood. 11 Moab hath been at ease from his youth, and he hath settled on his lees, and hath not been emptied from vessel to vessel, neither hath he gone into captivity: therefore his taste remained in him, and his scent is not changed. 12 Therefore, behold, the days come, saith the Lord, that I will send unto him wanderers, that shall cause him to wander, and shall empty his vessels, and break their bottles.

48.1-12 Moab. What an amazing people these Moabites. They actually magnified themselves against the Lord. They were insolent, their contempt, their lies, their pride, their arrogance, and their haughtiness bring their judgment on themselves. The judgment causes Jeremiah to howl (31). They had been allowed to remain in their land and were "settled upon their lees". This term has to do with wine that is not strained or processed. Moab would soon be poured out and broken by Babylon. Moab ceased to exist with the conquest of Nebuchadnezzar, just as Philistia had. Furthermore, anyone who refuses to join in the extirpation is cursed (10). To leave this people alive is to be deceitful (negligent) in God's eyes. Later this area was occupied by the Nabateans and flourished again before being incorporated into the Empire by the Romans.

48.13-47 And Moab shall be ashamed of Chemosh, as the house of Israel was ashamed of Bethel their confidence. 14 How say ye, We are mighty and strong men for the war? 15 Moab is spoiled, and gone up out of her cities, and his chosen young men are gone down to the slaughter, saith the King, whose name is the Lord of hosts. 16 The calamity of Moab is near to come, and his affliction hasteth fast. 17 All ye that are about him, bemoan him; and all ye that know his name, say, How is the strong staff broken, and the beautiful rod! 18 Thou daughter that dost inhabit Dibon, come down from thy

glory, and sit in thirst; for the spoiler of Moab shall come upon thee, and he shall destroy thy strong holds. 19 O inhabitant of Aroer, stand by the way, and espy; ask him that fleeth, and her that escapeth, and say, What is done? 20 Moab is confounded; for it is broken down: howl and cry; tell ye it in Arnon, that Moab is spoiled, 21 And judgment is come upon the plain country; upon Holon, and upon Jahazah, and upon Mephaath, 22 And upon Dibon, and upon Nebo, and upon Bethdiblathaim, 23 And upon Kiriathaim, and upon Bethgamul, and upon Bethmeon, 24 And upon Kerioth, and upon Bozrah, and upon all the cities of the land of Moab, far or near. 25 The horn of Moab is cut off, and his arm is broken, saith the Lord. 26 Make ye him drunken: for he magnified himself against the Lord: Moab also shall wallow in his vomit, and he also shall be in derision. 27 For was not Israel a derision unto thee? was he found among thieves? for since thou spakest of him, thou skippedst for joy. 28 O ye that dwell in Moab, leave the cities, and dwell in the rock, and be like the dove that maketh her nest in the sides of the hole's mouth. 29 We have heard the pride of Moab, (he is exceeding proud) his loftiness, and his arrogancy, and his pride, and the haughtiness of his heart. 30 I know his wrath, saith the Lord; but it shall not be so; his lies shall not so effect it. 31 Therefore will I howl for Moab, and I will cry out for all Moab; mine heart shall mourn for the men of Kirheres. 32 O vine of Sibmah, I will weep for thee with the weeping of Jazer: thy plants are gone over the sea, they reach even to the sea of Jazer: the spoiler is fallen upon thy summer fruits and upon thy vintage. 33 And joy and gladness is taken from the plentiful field, and from the land of Moab, and I have caused wine to fail from the winepresses: none shall tread with shouting; their shouting shall be no shouting. 34 From the cry of Heshbon even unto

Elealeh, and even unto Jahaz, have they uttered their voice, from Zoar even unto Horonaim, as an heifer of three years old: for the waters also of Nimrim shall be desolate. 35 Moreover I will cause to cease in Moab, saith the Lord, him that offereth in the high places, and him that burneth incense to his gods. 36 Therefore mine heart shall sound for Moab like pipes, and mine heart shall sound like pipes for the men of Kirheres: because the riches that he hath gotten are perished. 37 For every head shall be bald, and every beard clipped: upon all the hands shall be cuttings, and upon the loins sackcloth. 38 There shall be lamentation generally upon all the housetops of Moab, and in the streets thereof: for I have broken Moab like a vessel wherein is no pleasure, saith the Lord. 39 They shall howl, saying, How is it broken down! how hath Moab turned the back with shame! so shall Moab be a derision and a dismaying to all them about him. 40 For thus saith the Lord; Behold, he shall fly as an eagle, and shall spread his wings over Moab. 41 Kerioth is taken, and the strong holds are surprised, and the mighty men's hearts in Moab at that day shall be as the heart of a woman in her pangs. 42 And Moab shall be destroyed from being a people, because he hath magnified himself against the Lord. 43 Fear, and the pit, and the snare, shall be upon thee, O inhabitant of Moab, saith the Lord. 44 He that fleeth from the fear shall fall into the pit; and he that getteth up out of the pit shall be taken in the snare: for I will bring upon it, even upon Moab, the year of their visitation, saith the Lord. 45 They that fled stood under the shadow of Heshbon because of the force: but a fire shall come forth out of Heshbon, and a flame from the midst of Sihon, and shall devour the corner of Moab, and the crown of the head of the tumultuous ones. 46 Woe be unto thee, O Moab! the people of Chemosh perisheth: for thy sons are taken

captives, and thy daughters captives. 47 Yet will I bring again the captivity of Moab in the latter days, saith the Lord. Thus far is the judgment of Moab.

48.13-47 Nine times in this chapter it refers to "the Lord saith" or "thus saith the Lord". God informs this people that their God's will not deliver them anymore than the Golden calves delivered Israel. This is such a sad waste of prime young men. These specimens of the best of Moab are wasted when thrown against God. Men who could have made their nation proud are sacrificed in war for no profit. The strong staff is broken and the beautiful rod. Both staff (*mattaw*) and rod (*makkelaw*) speak of bearing fruit in a branch. This is the tragic loss of the prime young men of Moab. A call goes out to Dibon and Aroer, cities of Moab, to give up their young to the slaughter of war. The roll call of cities that will not escape the carnage continues. Halon, Jahazah, Mephaath, Dibon, Nero, Bethdiblathaim, Kirjathaim, Bethgamul and Bethmeon are listed as contributors to the river of lost humanity. So all the inhabitants of Moab who have magnified (made themselves great) themselves against God. They shall wallow in their own vomit and be in derision. Moab mocked Israel and laughed at her, so now Moab shall reap the same. Jeremiah howls for the vine of Sibmah, the loss of the fruit of the nation. The destruction of this nation is catalogued in great detail. The cities and areas are all included. Those that flee to the craggy heights of the mountains will not escape. Because of this complete and final judgment of Moab, Jeremiah sings and plays the death song (36). The final epitaph of Moab is God will break Moab like a vessel in which there is no pleasure (38). Moab shall be destroyed from being a people because he hath magnified himself against the Lord (42). As Jeremiah scans the landscape of world prophecy, he sees the scorched earth policy of God towards Moab. Smoke and ruins are all that remains of this once powerful people. So shall it be for every person and nation who magnify them self against God.

Chapter 49

49.1-6 Concerning the Ammonites, thus saith the Lord; Hath Israel no sons? hath he no heir? why then doth their king inherit Gad, and his people dwell in his cities? 2 Therefore, behold, the days come, saith the Lord, that I will cause an alarm of war to be heard in Rabbah of the Ammonites; and it shall be a desolate heap, and her daughters shall be burned with fire: then shall Israel be heir unto them that were his heirs, saith the Lord. 3 Howl, O Heshbon, for Ai is spoiled: cry, ye daughters of Rabbah, gird you with sackcloth; lament, and run to and fro by the hedges; for their king shall go into captivity, and his priests and his princes together. 4 Wherefore gloriest thou in the valleys, thy flowing valley, O backsliding daughter? that trusted in her treasures, saying, Who shall come unto me? 5 Behold, I will bring a fear upon thee, saith the Lord God of hosts, from all those that be about thee; and ye shall be driven out every man right forth; and none shall gather up him that wandereth. 6 And afterward I will bring again the captivity of the children of Ammon, saith the Lord.

49.1-6 Ammon. Ammon like Moab in the previous chapter was descended from Lot and the incestuous relationship with his own daughter. This nation will also cease to exist when overrun by Nebuchadnezzar. Ammon, together with Moab, were twin people in their treatment of Israel. They had oppressed Israel for eighteen years during the time of the judges. They had fought against Ephraim, Benjamin and Judah (Ju 10.7). They warred against Saul at Jabesh-gilead. They disrespected the ambassadors of David. Joab defeated them, and Jehoshaphat fought them. They took land from Israel after Tiglath-pileser ravaged the land. Ammon had taken possession of the inheritance of Israel and dwelt in the cities of Israel. Ammon was trusting in her riches and natural resources to protect her from conquest. These things would not assuage the anger of God, nor the vengeance of Nebuchadnezzar.

49.7-22 Concerning Edom, thus saith the Lord of hosts; Is wisdom no more in Teman? is counsel perished from the prudent? is their wisdom vanished? 8 Flee ye, turn back, dwell deep, O inhabitants of Dedan; for I will bring the calamity of Esau upon him, the time that I will visit him. 9 If grapegatherers come to thee, would they not leave some gleaning grapes? if thieves by night, they will destroy till they have enough. 10 But I have made Esau bare, I have uncovered his secret places, and he shall not be able to hide himself: his seed is spoiled, and his brethren, and his neighbours, and he is not. 11 Leave thy fatherless children, I will preserve them alive; and let thy widows trust in me. 12 For thus saith the Lord; Behold, they whose judgment was not to drink of the cup have assuredly drunken; and art thou he that shall altogether go unpunished? thou shalt not go unpunished, but thou shalt surely drink of it. 13 For I have sworn by myself, saith the Lord, that Bozrah shall become a desolation, a reproach, a waste, and a curse; and all the cities thereof shall be perpetual wastes. 14 I have heard a rumour from the Lord, and an ambassador

is sent unto the heathen, saying, Gather ye together, and come against her, and rise up to the battle. 15 For, lo, I will make thee small among the heathen, and despised among men. 16 Thy terribleness hath deceived thee, and the pride of thine heart, O thou that dwellest in the clefts of the rock, that holdest the height of the hill: though thou shouldest make thy nest as high as the eagle, I will bring thee down from thence, saith the Lord. 17 Also Edom shall be a desolation: every one that goeth by it shall be astonished, and shall hiss at all the plagues thereof. 18 As in the overthrow of Sodom and Gomorrah and the neighbour cities thereof, saith the Lord, no man shall abide there, neither shall a son of man dwell in it. 19 Behold, he shall come up like a lion from the swelling of Jordan against the habitation of the strong: but I will suddenly make him run away from her: and who is a chosen man, that I may appoint over her? for who is like me? and who will appoint me the time? and who is that shepherd that will stand before me? 20 Therefore hear the counsel of the Lord, that he hath taken against Edom; and his purposes, that he hath purposed against the inhabitants of Teman: Surely the least of the flock shall draw them out: surely he shall make their habitations desolate with them. 21 The earth is moved at the noise of their fall, at the cry the noise thereof was heard in the Red sea. 22 Behold, he shall come up and fly as the eagle, and spread his wings over Bozrah: and at that day shall the heart of the mighty men of Edom be as the heart of a woman in her pangs.

49.7-22 Edom. By man's standard Esau's descendants were very high and secure. By God's standard, they were just another foolish pride to be cast down. The almighty lets them know his battle with them will leave no prisoners and give no quarter. Thieves or robbers would not utterly destroy; they would only take the valuables. God needs no valuables. God is not there to plunder. If men were gathering grapes, they would leave some behind. God has no such intentions. God has tolerated this feud with Edom for generations and now the judgment falls. One of the most poetic and focused moments in scripture is penned by an unknown author in an unknown time. "How are the things of Esau searched out?" (Obadiah 1.4-6). The original language speaks of secret things. This goes far beyond visible things. Esau is about to be removed forever. The only thing left will be a vague memory of a once proud people.

49.23-27 Concerning Damascus. Hamath is confounded, and Arpad: for they have heard evil tidings: they are fainthearted; there is sorrow on the sea; it cannot be quiet. 24 Damascus is waxed feeble, and turneth herself to flee, and fear hath seized on her: anguish and sorrows have taken her, as a woman in travail. 25 How is the city of praise not left, the city of my joy! 26 Therefore her young men shall fall in her streets, and all the men of war shall be cut off in that day, saith the Lord of hosts. 27 And I will kindle a fire in the wall of Damascus, and it shall consume the palaces of Benhadad.

49.23-27 Damascus. The coming flood of Babylonian devastation will engulf Damascus as well. The picture here by Jeremiah is one of horror. It is of a wide-eyed woman who sees this tsunami about to break over Damascus and turns to run, but it is too late. This city has been of little impact for the last 100 years, so the mention here is brief. The Aramaean Kings had raided the villages of Israel (Amos 1.3-5), and now the tables will be reversed. The decades of decline concerning Damascus have erased the deeds of Damascus in the minds of men, but not in the memory of God. Like wine fermenting, the judgment of God on this wicked people has been seething since the days of Elisha's ministry. Damascus is past her prime, she is feeble, she turns to flee, but God has not forgot, and her flight is in vain. Since the day when Ahab made alliance with the King of Assyria who besieged Damascus, this city has been out of the eye of the Bible. For all these years we have heard nothing until now. It will yet surface again in our Bible when the world's greatest missionary, Paul, will be converted there and baptized. With the fruit of it's ill fated past now ripe to be harvested, God will concede to this storied city the great honor of the conversion of Paul, the Apostle to the Gentiles.

49.28-33 Concerning Kedar, and concerning the kingdoms of Hazor, which Nebuchadrezzar king of Babylon shall smite, thus saith the Lord; Arise ye, go up to Kedar, and spoil the men of the east. 29 Their tents and their flocks shall they take away: they shall take to themselves their curtains, and all their vessels, and their camels; and they shall cry unto them, Fear is on every side. 30 Flee, get you far off, dwell deep, O ye inhabitants of Hazor, saith the Lord; for Nebuchadrezzar king of Babylon hath taken counsel against you, and hath conceived a purpose against you. 31 Arise, get you up unto the wealthy nation, that dwelleth without care, saith the Lord, which have neither gates nor bars, which dwell alone. 32 And their camels shall be a booty, and the multitude of their cattle a spoil: and I will scatter into all winds them that are in the utmost corners; and I will bring their calamity from all sides thereof, saith the Lord. 33 And Hazor shall be a dwelling for dragons, and a desolation for ever: there shall no man abide there, nor any son of man dwell in it.

49.28-33 Kedar and Hazor. This prophecy consists of two

concise strophes. The funeral song of the nations includes this brief verse about the Arabians. They are admonished to flee while they can for their dwelling shall become a desolation. These people lived east of Palestine in the desert regions of Arabia. The swath of the army of Babylon will sweep through this area also. Because their wealth was in cattle and camels, they can escape and survive. The life of the true Bedouin in this part of the world has insured their survival. They are not tethered to the land by vineyards and permanent dwellings. Their mobility has given them the means of survival in the hot desert winds of war.

49.34-39 The word of the Lord that came to Jeremiah the prophet against Elam in the beginning of the reign of Zedekiah king of Judah, saying, 35 Thus saith the Lord of hosts; Behold, I will break the bow of Elam, the chief of their might. 36 And upon Elam will I bring the four winds from the four quarters of heaven, and will scatter them toward all those winds; and there shall be no nation whither the outcasts of Elam shall not come. 37 For I will cause Elam to be dismayed before their enemies, and before them that seek their life: and I will bring evil upon them, even my fierce anger, saith the Lord; and I will send the sword after them, till I have consumed them: 38 And I will set my throne in Elam, and will destroy from thence the king and the princes, saith the Lord. 39 But it shall come to pass in the latter days, that I will bring again the captivity of Elam, saith the Lord.

49.34-39 Elam. This is another example of Jeremiah using chiastic prophecy. This was spoken in the days of Zedekiah. Elam refers to the Persian legacy. This area has a long history. They are the descendants of Shem according to Josephus. This area would be significant in the Empire of the Medes and the Persians in the future. Is 22.6 lets us know that Elam served under Sennacherib when he besieged Jerusalem. The inclusion of this historical footnote here in this chapter seems out of place in the text. Possibly Jeremiah adds it as a footnote to express the breadth and scope of the conquest of the coming Babylonian army. As in most prophecy that Jeremiah speaks, God attacks a nations strength, never their weakness. Men seek weak openings. God always opposes at the strongest virtue. These Elamites were renowned for the skill at archery, so God says He will break their bow. The expression "four winds" speaks of military might God musters against His enemies (Ez 37.9, Dan 8.8). The establishment of the throne in Elam was fulfilled in Nebuchadnezzar, Cyrus, (Dan 8.2), and later when Alexander the Great subdued the region. It was here Alexander would die at the young age of 33.

Chapter 50

50.1 The word that the Lord spake against Babylon and against the land of the Chaldeans by Jeremiah the prophet.

50.1. Babylon. Just the mention of the word conjures vivid images. The bloodlust of world conquerors. Marching armies and nations left in rabble and ruin. Wealth beyond comprehension married to world power and dominance. Arrogance and pride on display. The sediment of false religion left behind. The legacy that remains and continues in so many religious falsehoods. The resurgence in the book of Revelations proves Babylon is not dead. Babylon is alive and growing. Here Jeremiah turns his final attention to Babylon before he closes his prophecy forever. Jeremiah has much to say about mighty, wicked, enduring Babylon. Babylon was one of the great world powers along with Egypt, Assyria, Media-Persia, Greece and Rome. Babylon is too important to briefly mention, so Jeremiah elaborates in detail. He gives two full chapters to the foremost power of his day.

50.2-8 Declare ye among the nations, and publish, and set up a standard; publish, and conceal not: say, Babylon is taken, Bel is confounded, Merodach is broken in pieces;

her idols are confounded, her images are broken in pieces. 3 For out of the north there cometh up a nation against her, which shall make her land desolate, and none shall dwell therein: they shall remove, they shall depart, both man and beast. 4 In those days, and in that time, saith the Lord, the children of Israel shall come, they and the children of Judah together, going and weeping: they shall go, and seek the Lord their God. 5 They shall ask the way to Zion with their faces thitherward, saying, Come, and let us join ourselves to the Lord in a perpetual covenant that shall not be forgotten. 6 My people hath been lost sheep: their shepherds have caused them to go astray, they have turned them away on the mountains: they have gone from mountain to hill, they have forgotten their restingplace. 7 All that found them have devoured them: and their adversaries said, We offend not, because they have sinned against the Lord, the habitation of justice, even the Lord, the hope of their fathers. 8 Remove out of the midst of Babylon, and go forth out of the land of the Chaldeans, and be as the he goats before the flocks.

50.2-8 Restoration. There is a two fold meaning here. First there is the restoration from the 70-year captivity. Secondly, there is the final restoration in the end times. The dichotomy here is that Babylon was destroyed and has never again existed as a physical place again, but in the nether world Babylon has never ceased to exist and be a constant wicked influence.

50.9-16 For, lo, I will raise and cause to come up against Babylon an assembly of great nations from the north country: and they shall set themselves in array against her; from thence she shall be taken: their arrows shall be as of a mighty expert man; none shall return in vain. 10 And Chaldea shall be a spoil: all that spoil her shall be satisfied, saith the Lord. 11 Because ye were glad, because ye rejoiced, O ye destroyers of mine heritage, because ye are grown fat as the heifer at grass, and bellow as bulls; 12 Your mother shall be sore confounded; she that bare you shall be ashamed: behold, the hindermost of the nations shall be a wilderness, a dry land, and a desert. 13 Because of the wrath of the Lord it shall not be inhabited, but it shall be wholly desolate: every one that goeth by Babylon shall be astonished, and hiss at all her plagues. 14 Put yourselves in array against Babylon round about: all ye that bend the bow, shoot at her, spare no arrows: for she hath sinned against the Lord. 15 Shout against her round about: she hath given her hand: her foundations are fallen, her walls are thrown down: for it is the vengeance of the Lord: take vengeance upon her; as she hath done, do unto her. 16 Cut off the sower from Babylon, and him that handleth the sickle in the time of harvest: for fear of the oppressing sword they shall turn every one to his people, and they shall flee every one to his own land.

50.9-16 Judgment of Babylon. Even though Babylon was the tool of God's vengeance, she does not escape the judgment upon herself. Her usefulness to achieve God's will does not recuse her. Babylon did not recognize it was God who gave her the prominence and wealth she enjoyed. Babylon mistook divine favor for human ability. God lifted Babylon up, and it would be God who brought her down. God sets Babylon up as a target for future conquest. The same awe she inspired in world dominance will now be felt by others at her demise and destruction.

50.17-32 Israel is a scattered sheep; the lions have driven him away: first the king of Assyria hath devoured him; and last this Nebuchadrezzar king of Babylon hath broken his bones. 18 Therefore thus saith the Lord of hosts, the God of Israel; Behold, I will punish the king of Babylon and his land, as I have punished the king of Assyria. 19 And I will bring Israel again to his habitation, and he shall feed on Carmel and Bashan, and his soul shall be satisfied upon mount Ephraim and Gilead. 20 In those days, and in that time, saith the Lord, the iniquity of Israel shall be sought for, and there shall be none; and the sins of Judah, and they shall not be found: for I will pardon them whom I reserve. 21 Go up against the land of Merathaim, even against it, and against the inhabitants of Pekod: waste and utterly destroy after them, saith the Lord, and do according to all that I have commanded thee. 22 A sound of battle is in the land, and of great destruction. 23 How is the hammer of the whole earth cut asunder and broken! how is Babylon become a desolation among the nations! 24 I have laid a snare for thee, and thou art also taken, O Babylon, and thou wast not aware: thou art found, and also caught, because thou hast striven against the Lord. 25 The Lord hath opened his armoury, and hath brought forth the weapons of his indignation: for this is the work of the Lord God of hosts in the land of the Chaldeans. 26 Come against her from the utmost border, open her storehouses: cast her up as heaps, and destroy her utterly: let nothing of her be left. 27 Slay all her bullocks; let them go down to the slaughter: woe unto them! for their day is come, the time of their visitation. 28 The voice of them that flee and escape out of the land of Babylon, to declare in Zion the vengeance of the Lord our God, the vengeance of his temple.

29 Call together the archers against Babylon: all ye that bend the bow, camp against it round about; let none thereof escape: recompense her according to her work; according to all that she hath done, do unto her: for she

hath been proud against the Lord, against the Holy One of Israel. 30 Therefore shall her young men fall in the streets, and all her men of war shall be cut off in that day, saith the Lord. 31 Behold, I am against thee, O thou most proud, saith the Lord God of hosts: for thy day is come, the time that I will visit thee. 32 And the most proud shall stumble and fall, and none shall raise him up: and I will kindle a fire in his cities, and it shall devour all round about him.

50.17-32 The hammer. The tool God used for judgment on so many nations is now turned to smash Babylon. God opens His armory and brings out His weapons. This was music to the ears of those captives in Babylon. Those who had felt the iron heel of this mighty nation could find solace in knowing her day would come. In a few short years Cyrus would sweep in and Babylon would meet it's fate. In 539 BC the Neo-Babylonian Empire was conquered by Cyrus the Great.

50.33-46 Thus saith the Lord of hosts; The children of Israel and the children of Judah were oppressed together: and all that took them captives held them fast; they refused to let them go. 34 Their Redeemer is strong; the Lord of hosts is his name: he shall throughly plead their cause, that he may give rest to the land, and disquiet the inhabitants of Babylon. 35 A sword is upon the Chaldeans, saith the Lord, and upon the inhabitants of Babylon, and upon her princes, and upon her wise men. 36 A sword is upon the liars; and they shall dote: a sword is upon her mighty men; and they shall be dismayed. 37 A sword is upon their horses, and upon their chariots, and upon all the mingled people that are in the midst of her; and they shall become as women: a sword is upon her treasures; and they shall be robbed. 38 A drought is upon her waters; and they shall be dried up: for it is the land of graven images, and they are mad upon their idols. 39 Therefore the wild beasts of the desert with the wild beasts of the islands shall dwell there, and the owls shall dwell therein: and it shall be no more inhabited for ever; neither shall it be dwelt in from generation to generation. 40 As God overthrew Sodom and Gomorrah and the neighbour cities thereof, saith the Lord; so shall no man abide there, neither shall any son of man dwell therein. 41 Behold, a people shall come from the north, and a great nation, and many kings shall be raised up from the coasts of the earth. 42 They shall hold the bow and the lance: they are cruel, and will not shew mercy: their voice shall roar like the sea, and they shall ride upon horses, every one put in array, like a man to the battle, against thee, O daughter of Babylon. 43 The king of Babylon hath heard the report of them, and his hands waxed feeble: anguish took hold of him, and pangs as of a woman in travail. 44 Behold, he shall come up like a lion from the swelling of Jordan unto the habitation of the strong: but I will make them suddenly run away from her: and who is a chosen man, that I may appoint over her? for who is like me? and who will appoint me the time? and who is that shepherd that will stand before me? 45 Therefore hear ye the counsel of the Lord, that he hath taken against Babylon; and his purposes, that he hath purposed against the land of the Chaldeans: Surely the least of the flock shall draw them out: surely he shall make their habitation desolate with them. 46 At the noise of the taking of Babylon the earth is moved, and the cry is heard among the nations.

50.33-46 The divine redeemer. God shows his people that He is still pleading their cause. God informs them of the greater purpose of giving their land rest because they had not celebrated the years of jubilee, so God forced the issue of the land being rested as He had commanded. The lingering question in the minds of the people, including Habakkuk, was why did God allow the Babylonians to do this? The Babylonians were such a wicked people. Here God patiently explains His grander purpose. Babylon was a tool in His hand to achieve His greater purpose to give the Promised Land rest, and purge His people of their idolatry. The coming clamor quieted the turmoil in the minds and hearts of those in captivity. Many times God does not tell humanity why He acts as He does, but in this case, God gently informs his captives in Babylon why life has unfolded for them as it has. Possibly the seventy times the year of Jubilee was not celebrated every 50 years in the 3500 years of the Old Testament is now fulfilled in the seventy years of captivity. Babylon has served it's purpose in the grand scheme of God's plan.

Chapter 51

51.1-48 Thus saith the Lord; Behold, I will raise up against Babylon, and against them that dwell in the midst of them that rise up against me, a destroying wind; 2 And will send unto Babylon fanners, that shall fan her, and shall empty her land: for in the day of trouble they shall be against her round about. 3 Against him that bendeth let the archer bend his bow, and against him that lifteth himself up in his brigandine: and spare ye not her young men; destroy ye utterly all her host. 4 Thus the slain shall fall in the land of the Chaldeans, and they that are thrust through in her streets. 5 For Israel hath not been forsaken, nor Judah of his God, of the Lord of hosts; though their land was filled with sin against the Holy One of Israel. 6 Flee out of the midst of Babylon, and deliver every man his soul: be not cut off in her iniquity; for this is the time of the Lord's vengeance; he will render unto her a recompence. 7 Babylon hath been a golden cup in the Lord's hand, that made all the earth drunken: the nations have drunken of her wine; therefore the nations are mad. 8 Babylon is suddenly fallen and destroyed: howl for her; take balm for her pain, if so be she may be healed. 9 We would have healed Babylon, but she is not healed: forsake her, and let us go every one into his own country: for her judgment reacheth unto heaven, and is lifted up even to the skies. 10 The Lord hath brought forth our righteousness: come, and let us declare in Zion the work of the Lord our God. 11 Make bright the arrows; gather the shields: the Lord hath raised up the spirit of the kings of the Medes: for his device is against Babylon, to destroy it; because it is the vengeance of the Lord, the vengeance of his temple. 12 Set up the standard upon the walls of Babylon, make the watch strong, set up the watchmen, prepare the ambushes: for the Lord hath both devised and done that which he spake against the inhabitants of Babylon. 13 O thou that dwellest upon many waters, abundant in treasures, thine end is come, and the measure of thy covetousness. 14 The Lord of hosts hath sworn by himself, saying, Surely I will fill thee with men, as with caterpillers; and they shall lift up a shout against thee. 15 He hath made the earth by his power, he hath established the world by his wisdom, and hath stretched out the heaven by his understanding. 16 When he uttereth his voice, there is a multitude of waters in the heavens; and he causeth the vapours to ascend from the ends of the earth: he maketh lightnings with rain, and bringeth forth the wind out of his treasures. 17 Every man is brutish by his knowledge; every founder is confounded by the graven image: for his molten image is falsehood, and there is no breath in them. 18 They are vanity, the work of errors: in the time of their visitation they shall perish. 19 The portion of Jacob is not like them; for he is the former of all things: and Israel is the rod of his inheritance: the Lord of hosts is his name. 20 Thou art my battle axe and weapons of war: for with thee will I break in pieces the nations, and with thee will I destroy kingdoms; 21 And with thee will I break in pieces the horse and his rider; and with thee will I break in pieces the chariot and his rider; 22 With thee also will I break in pieces man and woman; and with thee will I break in pieces old and young; and with thee will I break in pieces the young man and the maid; 23 I will also break in pieces with thee the shepherd and his flock; and with thee will I break in pieces the husbandman and his yoke of oxen; and with thee will I break in pieces captains and rulers. 24 And I will render unto Babylon and to all the inhabitants of Chaldea all their evil that they have done in Zion in your sight, saith the Lord. 25 Behold, I am against thee, O destroying mountain, saith the Lord, which destroyest all the earth: and I will stretch out mine hand upon thee, and roll thee down from the rocks, and will make thee a burnt mountain. 26 And they shall not take of thee a stone for a corner, nor a stone for foundations; but thou shalt be desolate for ever, saith the Lord. 27 Set ye up a standard in the land, blow the trumpet among the nations, prepare the nations against her, call together against her the kingdoms of Ararat, Minni, and Ashchenaz; appoint a captain against her; cause the horses to come up as the rough caterpillers. 28 Prepare against her the nations with the kings of the Medes, the captains thereof, and all the rulers thereof, and all the land of his dominion. 29 And the land shall tremble and sorrow: for every purpose of the Lord shall be performed against Babylon, to make the land of Babylon a desolation without an inhabitant. 30 The mighty men of Babylon have forborn to fight, they have remained in their holds: their might hath failed; they became as women: they have burned her dwellingplaces; her bars are broken. 31 One post shall run to meet another, and one messenger to meet another, to shew the king of Babylon that his city is taken at one end, 32 And that the passages are stopped, and the reeds they have burned with fire, and the men of war are affrighted. 33 For thus saith the Lord of hosts, the God of Israel; The daughter of Babylon is like a threshingfloor, it is time to thresh her: yet a little while, and the time of her harvest shall come. 34 Nebuchadrezzar the king of Babylon hath devoured me, he hath crushed me, he hath made me an empty vessel, he hath swallowed me up like a dragon, he hath filled his belly with my delicates, he hath cast me out. 35 The violence done to me and to my flesh be upon Babylon, shall the inhabitant of Zion say; and my blood upon the inhabitants of Chaldea, shall Jerusalem say. 36 Therefore thus saith the Lord; Behold, I will plead thy cause, and take vengeance for thee; and I will dry up her sea, and make her springs dry. 37 And Babylon shall become heaps, a dwellingplace for dragons, an astonishment, and an hissing, without an inhabitant. 38 They shall roar together like lions: they shall yell as lions' whelps. 39 In their heat I will make their feasts, and I will make them drunken, that they may rejoice, and sleep a perpetual sleep, and not wake, saith the Lord. 40 I will bring them down like lambs to the slaughter, like rams with he goats. 41 How is Sheshach taken! and how is the praise of the whole earth surprised! how is Babylon become an astonishment among the nations! 42 The sea is come up upon Babylon: she is covered with the multitude of the waves thereof. 43 Her cities are a desolation, a dry land, and a wilderness, a land wherein no man dwelleth, neither doth any son of man pass thereby. 44 And I will punish Bel in Babylon, and I will bring forth out of his mouth that which he hath swallowed up: and the nations shall not flow together any more unto him: yea, the wall of Babylon shall fall. 45 My people, go ye out of the midst of her, and deliver ye every man his soul from the fierce anger of the Lord. 46 And lest your heart faint, and ye fear for the rumour that shall be heard in the land; a rumour shall both come one year, and after that in another year shall come a rumour, and violence in the land, ruler against ruler. 47 Therefore, behold, the days come, that I will do judgment upon the graven images of Babylon: and her whole land shall be confounded, and all her slain shall fall in the midst of her. 48 Then the heaven and the earth, and all that is therein, shall sing for Babylon: for the spoilers shall come unto her from the north, saith the Lord.

51.1-48 Utter destruction. Babylon hath been a golden cup in the Lord's hand that made all the earth drunken. This cryptogram is a two-fold prophecy. This is fulfilled in the destruction of Babylon and also in the end time during the time of great tribulation. The agent of her destruction will be the Medes. The destruction is detailed to many degrees. It is a complete destruction. As Babylon was the vessel in the hand of the lord to destroy many nations, so now the Medes will be the vessel against Babylon. The guards are set on the walls. As God sends lightening and rain, so will He send the storm against mighty Babylon. The graven images shall be brought down. Cyrus becomes the battle-axe of the Lord as Nebuchadnezzar once was. None of the debris of Babylon will ever be used to build upon again. The mighty men of Babylon refuse to fight. The madness of war Nebuchadnezzar unleashed on Judah will now be unleashed on Babylon itself. This proud land once so powerful will become nonexistent. Babylon is referred to as Sheshach. This is an *athbash*. An *athbash* is a cipher used in Jewish mystical and allegorical writing in which each letter of a word is replaced by that letter which stands as many places from the end of the Hebrew alphabet as the letter replaced stands from the beginning.

In verse 41 both words are used. The symbolism is clear; Babylon has been replaced in the hand of God by Cyrus. She who was the leader has now become the pursued. Truly the first shall be last.

51.49-58 As Babylon hath caused the slain of Israel to fall, so at Babylon shall fall the slain of all the earth. 50 Ye that have escaped the sword, go away, stand not still: remember the Lord afar off, and let Jerusalem come into your mind. 51 We are confounded, because we have heard reproach: shame hath covered our faces: for strangers are come into the sanctuaries of the Lord's house. 52 Wherefore, behold, the days come, saith the Lord, that I will do judgment upon her graven images: and through all her land the wounded shall groan. 53 Though Babylon should mount up to heaven, and though she should fortify the height of her strength, yet from me shall spoilers come unto her, saith the Lord. 54 A sound of a cry cometh from Babylon, and great destruction from the land of the Chaldeans: 55 Because the Lord hath spoiled Babylon, and destroyed out of her the great voice; when her waves do roar like great waters, a noise of their voice is uttered: 56 Because the spoiler is come upon her, even upon Babylon, and her mighty men are taken, every one of their bows is broken: for the Lord God of recompences shall surely requite. 57 And I will make drunk her princes, and her wise men, her captains, and her rulers, and her mighty men: and they shall sleep a perpetual sleep, and not wake, saith the King, whose name is the Lord of hosts. 58 Thus saith the Lord of hosts; The broad walls of Babylon shall be utterly broken, and her high gates shall be burned with fire; and the people shall labour in vain, and the folk in the fire, and they shall be weary.

51.49-58 The cause of Babylon's fall. Because Babylon treated the people of God with such barbaric, heartless disdain, they must now reap the consequences of their atrocities. We know from the book of Daniel that Babylon forced the people it conquered to adopt it's false religion. This will be true in the final days during the great tribulation as well.

1.59-64 The word which Jeremiah the prophet commanded Seraiah the son of Neriah, the son of Maaseiah, when he went with Zedekiah the king of Judah into Babylon in the fourth year of his reign. And this Seraiah was a quiet prince. 60 So Jeremiah wrote in a book all the evil that should come upon Babylon, even all these words that are written against Babylon. 61 And Jeremiah said to Seraiah, When thou comest to Babylon, and shalt see, and shalt read all these words; 62 Then shalt thou say, O Lord, thou hast spoken against this place, to cut it off, that none shall remain in it, neither man nor beast, but that it shall be desolate for ever. 63 And it shall be, when thou hast made an end of reading this book, that thou shalt bind a stone to it, and cast it into the midst of Euphrates: 64 And thou shalt say, Thus shall Babylon sink, and shall not rise from the evil that I will bring upon her: and they shall be weary. Thus far are the words of Jeremiah.

51.59-64 The book of Jeremiah. These events were recorded by Jeremiah long before they happened. Jeremiah gave them to Seraiah, one of the princes, and asked him to read it upon arriving in Babylon. Seraiah was to then bind it to a stone and cast it into the Euphrates river with the epitaph: Thus shall Babylon sink. Jeremiah, the true prophet, foretold these events years before they came to pass. Babylon had been arraigned, indicted, convicted and sentenced. Mighty Babylon, the Medo-Babylonian Empire that had ruled the entire fertile crescent and Arabia, is now defunct.

Chapter 52

52.1-11 Zedekiah was one and twenty years old when he began to reign, and he reigned eleven years in Jerusalem. And his mother's name was Hamutal the daughter of Jeremiah of Libnah. 2 And he did that which was evil in the eyes of the Lord, according to all that Jehoiakim had done. 3 For through the anger of the Lord it came to pass in Jerusalem and Judah, till he had cast them out from his presence, that Zedekiah rebelled against the king of Babylon. 4 And it came to pass in the ninth year of his reign, in the tenth month, in the tenth day of the month, that Nebuchadrezzar king of Babylon came, he and all his army, against Jerusalem, and pitched against it, and built forts against it round about. 5 So the city was besieged unto the eleventh year of king Zedekiah. 6 And in the fourth month, in the ninth day of the month, the famine was sore in the city, so that there was no bread for the people of the land. 7 Then the city was broken up, and all the men of war fled, and went forth out of the city by night by the way of the gate between the two walls, which was by the king's garden; (now the Chaldeans were by the city round about:) and they went by the way of the plain. 8 But the army of the Chaldeans pursued after the king, and overtook Zedekiah in the plains of Jericho; and all his army was scattered from him. 9 Then they took the king, and carried him up unto the king of Babylon to Riblah in the land of Hamath; where he gave judgment upon him. 10 And the king of Babylon slew the sons of Zedekiah before his eyes: he slew also all the princes of Judah in Riblah. 11 Then he put out the eyes of Zedekiah; and the king of Babylon bound him in chains, and carried him to Babylon, and put him in prison till the day of his death.

52.1-11 The fall of Jerusalem. It began with an eighteen-month siege. Zedekiah the king attempts to flee and is captured. His sons are put to death and his eyes are gouged out. Zedekiah is then given a living death by being cast into prison until the day he died. The king's life mirrors the fate of the nation as well. Judah could not escape the judgment, her sons were slaughtered and her spiritual eyes were put out. Judah was held captive until some things died in her. One thing that died in the seventy year incarceration was idolatry. After the restoration and repatriation we never again see Israel worshipping idols. This blight on her history for over one thousand years is finally overcome. The tragic price was the death of Jerusalem, here recorded in the last chapter of the great prophet Jeremiah.

52.12-23 Now in the fifth month, in the tenth day of the month, which was the nineteenth year of Nebuchadrezzar king of Babylon, came Nebuzaradan, captain of the guard, which served the king of Babylon, into Jerusalem, 13 And burned the house of the Lord, and the king's house; and all the houses of Jerusalem, and all the houses of the great men, burned he with fire: 14 And all the army of the Chaldeans, that were with the captain of the guard, brake down all the walls of Jerusalem round about. 15 Then Nebuzaradan the captain of the guard carried away

captive certain of the poor of the people, and the residue of the people that remained in the city, and those that fell away, that fell to the king of Babylon, and the rest of the multitude. 16 But Nebuzaradan the captain of the guard left certain of the poor of the land for vinedressers and for husbandmen. 17 Also the pillars of brass that were in the house of the Lord, and the bases, and the brasen sea that was in the house of the Lord, the Chaldeans brake, and carried all the brass of them to Babylon. 18 The caldrons also, and the shovels, and the snuffers, and the bowls, and the spoons, and all the vessels of brass wherewith they ministered, took they away. 19 And the basons, and the firepans, and the bowls, and the caldrons, and the candlesticks, and the spoons, and the cups; that which was of gold in gold, and that which was of silver in silver, took the captain of the guard away. 20 The two pillars, one sea, and twelve brasen bulls that were under the bases, which king Solomon had made in the house of the Lord: the brass of all these vessels was without weight. 21 And concerning the pillars, the height of one pillar was eighteen cubits; and a fillet of twelve cubits did compass it; and the thickness thereof was four fingers: it was hollow. 22 And a chapiter of brass was upon it; and the height of one chapiter was five cubits, with network and pomegranates upon the chapiters round about, all of brass. The second pillar also and the pomegranates were like unto these. 23 And there were ninety and six pomegranates on a side; and all the pomegranates upon the network were an hundred round about.

52.12-23 The temple. The proud building that had stood for over three hundred and fifty years and been the central place of worship for fifteen kings was now to die also. An anonymous Babylonian soldier lights a fire and sets this magnificent temple to the flame. This event is so moving the Bible includes a book of lamentations to record the trauma. The walls are broken down. The populace is rounded up and led away in chains. The Babylonians strip the valuable brass out of the temple. They gather up the vessels of gold and silver and take them as the spoil of war. Holy vessels that had been bathed in the glory and majesty of God for centuries became war booty. Babylon won the war against Judah, and the right to claim this bounty, but God would not forget Babylon. Within the span of forty eight years, in 539 BC, Cyrus would invade Babylon and bring the Neo-Babylonian Empire to its end.

52.24-30 And the captain of the guard took Seraiah the chief priest, and Zephaniah the second priest, and the three keepers of the door: 25 He took also out of the city an eunuch, which had the charge of the men of war; and seven men of them that were near the king's person, which were found in the city; and the principal scribe of the host, who mustered the people of the land; and threescore men of the people of the land, that were found in the midst of the city. 26 So Nebuzaradan the captain of the guard took them, and brought them to the king of Babylon to Riblah. 27 And the king of Babylon smote them, and put them to death in Riblah in the land of Hamath. Thus Judah was carried away captive out of his own land. 28 This is the people whom Nebuchadrezzar carried away captive: in the seventh year three thousand Jews and three and twenty: 29 In the eighteenth year of Nebuchadrezzar he carried away captive from Jerusalem eight hundred thirty and two persons: 30 In the three and twentieth year of Nebuchadrezzar Nebuzaradan the captain of the guard carried away captive of the Jews seven hundred forty and five persons: all the persons were four thousand and six hundred.

52.24-30 The captives. The Babylonians appear to cull through the populace and expiate them in several waves of captivity. Four thousand six hundred are listed as taken away. Judah is one king removed from Josiah and the greatest revival the nation ever experienced. How quickly one leader can influence a nation. Josiah took Judah to a spiritual high and his son took Judah to a spiritual low.

52.31-34 And it came to pass in the seven and thirtieth year of the captivity of Jehoiachin king of Judah, in the twelfth month, in the five and twentieth day of the month, that Evilmerodach king of Babylon in the first year of his reign lifted up the head of Jehoiachin king of Judah, and brought him forth out of prison. 32 And spake kindly unto him, and set his throne above the throne of the kings that were with him in Babylon, 33 And changed his prison garments: and he did continually eat bread before him all the days of his life. 34 And for his diet, there was a continual diet given him of the king of Babylon, every day a portion until the day of his death, all the days of his life.

52.31-34 Jehoiachin. There is a seemingly innocuous footnote about Jehoichin the king being released from prison. This is again a mirror showing how the king's fate signals the nation's fate. Judah will also yet be released from her captivity. It is the final pen stroke of this major prophet, after a lifetime of faithfully executing his charge to speak the Word of God faithfully. Few times in the history of the world has a man like Jeremiah appeared. The span of his vision is worldwide. He was faithful to his calling. His ministry spanned decades and kings. He knew great luxury and deep poverty. He experienced unparalleled spiritual highs and unspeakable human deprivations. He complained, he cried, he exulted joyfully, he was maligned, he was imprisoned, he was rescued, still he remained faithful to his calling. He left behind one of the greatest works of penmanship the world has ever seen. God in His infinite wisdom saw fit to only anoint four men as major prophets. Jeremiah is in that elite quartet. His voice was opposed at times, ignored and dissed often, but it will live forever, for the grass withers and the flower fades, but the Word of our God shall stand forever.

The Story Behind the Expository Series

This is a story about a man, his morals, and his ethics. The man's name was Millard Deramus. He was my paternal grandfather.

Millard lived at the end of a dirt and gravel road in Western Central Arkansas. When the road, as it was, reached his homestead, it turned and headed out of the woods. He was born a quarter of a mile from where he lived his entire life. I am not sure if he ever ventured out of the state of Arkansas. Possibly he got as far as a neighboring state once.

Many years ago he had a neighbor he simply referred to as Mr. Poole. One day Mr. Poole left. When it came time to pay the yearly taxes on their property, Mr. Poole had not returned. Millard was a good neighbor, so he did what he felt good neighbors do, he decided Mr. Poole's taxes should be paid so when Mr. Poole returned, he would not be in arrears with the state of Arkansas.

Millard hitched his mules and went on to Mr. Poole's land and cut a load of pulp wood and took it to the mill and sold it. He then went to the county seat and paid Mr. Poole's taxes. The next year Mr. Poole had still not returned, so Millard again cut pulp wood off Mr. Poole's land, sold it, and paid the taxes on Mr. Poole's land. This continued for many, many years. Mr. Poole never returned and each year my grandfather would cut timber off of Mr. Poole's land and sell it and pay the taxes on Mr. Poole's land.

I was there the day the attorney came to see Millard. We were on the back porch that had been screened in, and we were drinking coffee. I still have the two coffee cups we used that day. I heard the conversation from three feet away. The attorney had a briefcase full of papers he wanted Millard to sign.

The attorney informed Millard that according to the state of Arkansas, Millard was the owner of the 280 acres next door by the default of paying the taxes for the last 20 years. The name Millard Deramus was on every yearly receipt for over 20 years. The amount of money being discussed was substantial. I watched my grandfather closely. There was no reaction at all. No smile, not even a raised eyebrow.

Millard patiently waited for the attorney to finish. The attorney requested my grandfather sign the documents accepting ownership of 280 acres that joined his 70 acres. The value of the land at that time, including the timber, was well over a quarter of a million dollars. When the attorney finished and asked my grandfather to sign the documents he quietly and firmly said no, I will not sign. He informed the attorney that was not his land and he had never taken anything that did not belong to him in his life.

The amount of money was staggering to me. I was watching a man who had lived a simple rustic life for all of his eighty-plus years. He wore bib overalls and drove old pick-up trucks. When younger, he worked as a blacksmith out under the oak tree in his yard. I still have items he forged under that old oak tree. I watched that day as the attorney attempted to stoke the fire of avarice in Millard Deramus.

The attorney told Millard all he could do with several hundred thousand dollars. He floated the idea of a new home, a new truck, retirement, travel. Millard just stared at the attorney. No comment. None. The attorney tried again. Will you just sign, Millard? For your children? No comment. None. Finally the attorney asked, "Is there anything I can do to get you to sign these papers?" My grandfather simply shook his head no. He said one sentence. He said, "It ain't my land."

My grandfather died and was buried a short distance from where he lived his entire life. My grandmother (Dolly) lived a few more years. The children convinced her to sign the papers to claim ownership of the land because otherwise it would simply go back to the state. She signed, the land was sold, and my father was one of eight children who inherited.

When my father died I received my inheritance, part of which was the money from the sale of Mr. Poole's land. For a long time I pondered what to do. I did not feel like I could accept money I had witnessed my grandfather refuse on the afternoon on the back porch so many years before. So I waited. I did nothing. I never spent one dime of that money.

In 2016 an idea came to me that seemed an appropriate way to use that money. It is the money being used to produce the Expository Series. I did not know of any Apostolic writings that were doing an Expository Series. So I took that money and began to print books for Apostolic people to read.

The books of the Expository Series are printed without charge to the authors. The proceeds and profit of the books sold online go back into a non-profit fund to print more Apostolic books. None of the online profit is going to any personal use for anyone. If an author buys his book direct from wholesale after it is published and sells it, then he is welcomed to keep any profit from those sales.

I would like to thank all the men who have contributed their work to this endeavor. Scott Hall, Bart Adkins, Vaughn Reece, Kevin Archer, Ben Weeks, and Edward Seabrooks have all contributed. We have now published fifteen volumes and have three more to be published in the next sixty days. Others have also shown interest in publishing their works. Our goal is to have twenty volumes published by the end of 2017.

The publisher we are using has informed me we are their best seller they have ever published. We have now sold several thousand dollars of books since September 1, 2016. I am deeply grateful to everyone who has purchased our product.

Now you know the story behind the Expository Series. A simple Christian man with ethics and morals, opened his heart, and showed me his faith on a warm spring day, in a simple homestead, many years ago. Today I say thank you to my grandfather, Millard Deramus. Thank you for your ethics. Thank you for your morals. Thank you for your Christian faith.

May your memory be blessed and revered. You never travelled 100 miles from where you were born, but your legacy has spanned America.

www.ingramcontent.com/pod-product-compliance
Lightning Source LLC
Chambersburg PA
CBHW071728080526
44588CB00013B/1947